How to Find and Date

Table of Contents:

Introduction

Chapter 1...............Understanding the Female Psychology with Social Media

Chapter 2...............The Mindset and How to Build Confidence

Chapter 3...............Why Instagram is Better Than Using Dating Platforms

Chapter 4...............How to Maximize Your Profile for Attracting Women

Chapter 5...............How to Build Your Female Following Through Instagram

Chapter 6...............The Approach and How to Categorize Women

Chapter 7...............The Conversation

Chapter 8...............Closing on The Date

Ending Thoughts

Introduction

I remember when I was growing up the only way to date a girl was by walking up and asking her out. You had no choice; it was either approach her boldly or stay in your place and watch someone else who had the actual courage do it. If you did not have the courage to do it directly in person, you would write her a note and hope for the best. Back then there were no such thing as smart phones with high-speed internet to make it easily accessible to "virtually" approach a woman, except now in modern times dating has turned heavily towards the online path. When the concept of online dating came to fame, I remember how odd it felt meeting a potential girlfriend or fling online, I thought it was just as cliché as everyone else did. Except as time passed, I realized the internet has become a powerhouse within the dating community. The number of women you can potentially date are endless, and they are all right there at your fingertips. You may think I am talking about those popular dating apps and websites many use now a days, but I am not. I am talking about Instagram, one of the most widely used social media apps in the world. Instagram has millions of active users daily and that number is only increasing each day compared to the limited amount of people on dating platforms.

Before the internet, there was no such thing as dating platforms or social media. Everyone dated the people who lived within their area, school, or place of work. Now? It has exposed us to the world and everyone in it. It has given singles an infinite number of choices to choose from, and Instagram provides all you need to take full advantage of that. Over the past few years, I have found proven tactics that successfully leverage Instagram to increase your pipeline of women whether it is for serious relationships or casual dating. I have always been asked about the methods I use to find women off Instagram and how I get them on dates within days so often. Most people see social media as a platform for mingling with friends and family, but I see it as the best online dating opportunity. Believe me, messaging every woman you see is not the tactic, there are more calculated methods that are easy and quick to learn. I will be sharing my methods on how to understand women in a social media world, where to find them, how to approach them, and how to land a date with them. I will also give tips on dating and personal development that will help you tremendously for your future dates to come. With Instagram, you can choose who you want to approach instead of swiping right because she was the "best option" given to you at that moment. Swiping left and right, paying for extra features, and settling for what they give you should not be the main method you depend on to find dates. Follow the steps I am about to share with you, and I guarantee the pipeline of women in your life will double sooner than you think. Let us begin!

Disclaimer: *The contents of this book are suggestions based on first-hand experiences, observations, and theories. Anything related to gender or dating should be taken as a generalization, not a fact for every single person. The results are contingent on your patience, effort, and desire to follow the contents within this book. Some foul language is sparingly used throughout the book, reader beware.*

Chapter 1: Understanding the Female Psychology with Social Media

One thing we know is women will always be women. They are sensitive, attention loving, emotional human beings with the same feminine instincts since before the birth of social media. They have become obsessed with beauty and image, always competing with one another to be the most glamorous or the most desired by men. Except before social media, that was on a much smaller scale, it was always within their group of friends, coworkers, or even family. Now? They feel as if they are competing with thousands trying to do the exact same thing. It went from trying to be the most desired girl in town to the most desired girl on the internet. Everything a woman was accustomed to when it came to image and dating drastically blew up. That one guy at the store who gave her a compliment now turned into hundreds doing the same in the form of likes and comments. Being asked out on a date once or twice a week turned into ten times a day in her inbox. Instead of having one admirer they now have hundreds if not thousands now following them online. At first it was new and exciting, but as time passed, all the newfound attention became the standard. Now their image is heavily based on how many followers they have, the attention they get online, or the glamorous lifestyle they can show off to the world. Social media is a huge factor in their self-esteem and how they value their femininity whether they want to admit it or not. Many feel embarrassed when they post and do not receive the attention they expected. Because in their mind, they failed to gain the approval of the public and of the men showing other women more attention than them. As a result, they compare themselves to the girl who looks prettier or the one all the men drool over because she has spent thousands of dollars enhancing her physique. They will measure their appearance feeling sufficient or inadequate depending on how they compare. We do not live in the world where we idolized that one actress or model based on her natural beauty and feminine glow like before. We live in a world where beauty is constantly being enhanced, and many are chasing the same image due to the new beauty standards society has now set for women.

Women know they are put on a pedestal as a sex symbol by society and thrive on that attention and image. As social media became more popular, they began using it to economical or emotional advantage. Fast forward to now, you see more women exposing themselves daily for likes or soliciting their bodies by charging money in exchange for sexual videos or pictures. The amount of attention women get via social media is enormous whether they are Instafamous or not. Ironically, you would think their confidence is through the roof, but it is not when you take a closer look. Most females have become obsessed with the need to be wanted by everyone so they can feel beautiful or sexy. The more likes, comments, and messages, the more vibrant they feel. But the moment they receive less attention, they begin to feel ugly and inferior. That is why so many women have low self-esteem now and fear the loss of that consistent validation so they can feel good about themselves on a continual basis. That is the reason the typical profile of a woman is full of ass and cleavage pictures, they know that is what men like, so they reciprocate the same exact posts repeatedly to achieve that psychological dependency of feeling wanted. They are too busy trying to compete with one another to be the worlds most wanted woman thinking they are not pretty enough if they see someone else with more body or attention than themselves. So as a byproduct, they have developed this form of synthetic social media confidence to mask what happens within their emotional core due to the pressures of society. Although their subconscious is consistently attacking their self-perceived image, many have learned how to hide it and display a fake persona as if their self-assurance is unbreakable. Except many have a hard time dealing with it deep down.

Why is this important to know?

If you want to date loads of beautiful women, you must realize that they are people just like you and I because at the end of it all, social media is an illusion. Without it, every single person is just a regular human being. A lot of men see a woman with a hot body and a few thousand followers as if she is untouchable and act like a fan. They either avoid approaching her or they show excessive amounts of attention like other men thinking that is the best way to get noticed. That is the furthest thing from the truth because viewing them in that sense only feeds into their validation and never gives you a shot in hell with anyone worthwhile. You see, when you form the proper perspective with women, there is not one female that can hinder your self-assurance as a man and your ability to approach them online or in person.

After reading this book, you will know how to stand out from the rest of the men who act like fan boys while you show high value instead. You will not see any woman as above or below you, but as an equal by desensitizing her beauty and social status on an app. Too many men miss out on amazing dates or relationships because they place women above them demonstrating low value, and that stops now. The more confidence and high value you portray to women, the more you will attract. The more fear you show and the more desperation you portray, the less you will attract, it is as simple as that. See her as a normal human being just like you and I, that will be the best way to start forming that proper perspective. Mastering this will give you a better empathetic viewpoint and a lot less fear interacting with them in general. At the end of the day, women are people with feelings and emotions too, so never be scared to approach or talk to women because of how beautiful they are or how stuck up they look on Instagram. You must see through their beauty, because they can be just as nervous or scared to speak to you too, they just know how to hide it better. So, remember, the proper perspective with women will always be key and understanding how women think with social media will help tremendously.

Chapter 2: The Mindset and How to Build Confidence

Women are tricky to fully figure out sometimes, we all know that. As I mentioned before about their insecurities with image, women also have an abundance mindset with men at the same time. They might be comparing themselves to other women thinking they are not pretty enough to society at times, but they are also not scared to drop a man within seconds and move on to the next one. I know, it is confusing but keep in mind that although women have insecurities about their image, many still carry high standards and expectations when it comes to dating and relationships. If you pay close attention to how women interact and handle men and adopt that same mentality, you are already one step ahead of most men out there whether you are dating or in a relationship.

What men need to understand is no matter what, women will always get a lot of attention from men on a consistent basis. Men have always been instinctually the seed spreaders and the chasers, while women have always been the nurturers and the choosers. How many times have you seen a woman make a gameplan with her girlfriends to go to a bar and approach as many men as possible to bet who can bring one home first? Or have contests with each other to see how many men they can sleep with within a year and list the names in a notebook? Most likely never. If you think about it, it is always the men chasing their women, and the woman choosing their men. Yes, a woman can say she likes you and ask to hang out but guess what? That is because she *chose* you and is most likely assertive with what she wants. If a man is asked out by ten different women who are attractive, he will most likely say yes, to all ten women. But on the contrary, if a woman is asked out by ten different men who are attractive, she will say no to eight or nine out of those ten men. Females already have the mindset of abundance with dating even if they have their own insecurities set aside, it is called standards and having value in yourself. Just because you have certain insecurities about yourself does not mean you cannot have self-assurance in other aspects either. Since men are known as the chasers, it solidifies women with that feeling of assurance that there will always be another man waiting to ask her out. Meaning she will wait for the one she wants to yes to as she continues to turn other men down in the meantime. Even male celebrities have been caught in the inbox of your average girl who is not even famous, but you never see the same situation with a celebrity woman to a man. It is a standard that women have set themselves to when it comes to men, and they know it will not change anytime soon. You can look like a Calvin Klein model or a scrub, and a woman with value will never be scared to call it quits with you. Attractive women know they have numerous amounts of men in their inbox who are willing to jump on the snap of their finger, and they know there will always be more down the line. Which is why you must have the same abundance mentality from the beginning as well, you need to mirror that assurance women have knowing your options are endless. Yes, women may get more attention on average than men, but demonstrating you know your worth will only help you attract more women. If a woman walks into the room with the energy of a queen and you see she turns heads, then you need to walk into the room with the energy of a king to turn heads as well. By that I do not mean being arrogant, cocky, or full of yourself, that is a direct sign of insecurity and women will pick up on that fast. What I mean is others will perceive you the exact same way you perceive yourself, never forget that. Whether it is in pictures or in person, you must show you are secure with yourself and that nothing will break that no matter what.

Improve Your Life and Confidence Will Come

To gain confidence in life and dating, you need to instill a high level of self-worth in your head. Your brain might be made of only tissue and nerves, but it controls your whole body and emotions. Many men lack confidence in various aspects of their life due to not knowing what needs to be done to obtain it. You need to implant a positive, unified thought process in your mind with goals to successfully attract what you want out of life and dating. Your Health, finances, and mental state should be your top priority. Having those three things in check will drastically improve your confidence naturally if you are constantly working to better yourself in each aspect. Each of these three aspects will always have another level to reach, even if you think you are the strongest mentally, the fittest, or the wealthiest. There will always be another level to achieve and more to tweak and improve on. There will times where you feel as if you are plateauing or complacent in each of the three aspects, and that is when you know you need to make a change to reach that next level. So, let's go over the three aspects in detail.

Health

A healthy lifestyle means more energy and a prolonged life. You need to take your health seriously by taking vitamins daily and exercise at least three to four times a week. If you prefer not to be a gym rat, at least find something active to do so you can get a good sweat in and gain endurance. But most of all, never forget to watch your diet. Eating chips and fast food everyday will only make you feel lethargic and bloated all the time. Being conscious of what you put in your body will help you internally and externally making you look healthy and feel great. You do not have to meal prep as if you are competing in a bodybuilding show but always avoid overly processed foods with high saturated fat and drink plenty of water. As I mentioned before and will continue to mention, the overall energy you give off is everything. If you feel good, you will look good, and the people around you will perceive you the exact same way. But if you feel sluggish and look out of shape, people will see you the exact same way as well. Being healthy along with looking healthy will cause you to view yourself as more attractive leading to a better appearance overall boosting your confidence.

Finances

Finances are important whether you want to believe it or not. A lot of people say money isn't everything, but it does solve a lot of issues. Women have always instinctually looked for the strongest, hardest working, most well-rounded male because they want someone who will be a provider and a leader for her and their children. It is the same concept with most animal species on the planet, females choose the alpha of the pack to mate with because to them, it will give their offspring the highest chance of survival. That same concept applies to us as humans, just in our own way. If you are established financially, it automatically increases attraction because it shows her two key things, stability and high status. But to be clear, it is not about how much money you make to them; it is the security standpoint of it all. Of course, each woman has her own idea of what security is, but what does a man with any sort of security show? Ambition, work ethic, and determination just like an alpha. It shows that if she stays and you end up having a family, she will not worry where her children's next meal will come from or if they will have a roof over their head. Although that is jumping way ahead, I am only trying to demonstrate the psychological aspect of how women instinctually view an established man. Which is why you tend to see a wealthy man as absolute chick magnet, women see him as a high-status male, and it attracts them. Yes, there are gold diggers out there, but those are obvious to pick out because they only want expensive things and will only go on expensive dates. Not everyone reading this book will become filthy rich or even want to become that wealthy, but the main goal is to make enough money so you can feel *free*. The freedom of not having to search for the cheapest item on the menu or clothing rack. Or the feeling of never having to turn down a great date opportunity or memorable experience because you are tight on bills. That is the mission, to feel free without limitation. When you obtain success and freedom, you will feel proud of yourself and of your accomplishments boosting your confidence dramatically, believe me when I tell you that. That is why you must make it a goal to improve your finances. Get a second job, start a business, study a skill or get a higher degree. All of that will get you on your way to being financially secure and have that weight lifted off your shoulders. It does not matter if you are over thirty years old or just starting college, it is never too late to improve your finances. As you see yourself improving becoming more established, just that alone will bring you more confidence because the journey itself feels just as good as the end result.

Mental State

For your mental state, read or listen to books on all the things you want to learn or improve on. Reading for me changed my life, I have learned so many new things that have helped me gain knowledge and wisdom on so many different subjects. Knowledge is the most valuable aspect in naturally gaining confidence hands down. How do you think all these self-made multi-millionaires and billionaires became so successful? They spent years reading and educating themselves constantly applying that new knowledge to their careers and relationships. They read and educate themselves on everything that will help them achieve their goals, and a well-educated person will naturally be more confident overall. The more you learn, the more you can apply that knowledge every day and improve on everything you want to work on. For example, if you have unhealthy thought processes such as self-sabotage or depression, look into subjects such as neurolinguistic programing (NLP). Neurolinguistic programming is designed to help you rewire your brain and solidify new thought processes in your head using proven techniques. NLP is how all these big-time motivational speakers and self-help gurus learned to change so many lives, they are all experts in NLP and psychology in general. If you want to strengthen your leadership skills, get books on leadership. Then read the biographies of the biggest leaders of world history and I bet you will learn a lot from them. If you want to learn how to be a better speaker or conversationalist, grab a few books on how to sharpen your communication skills and so forth. In all, there are books on so many subjects, but my biggest recommendation is to read books on all of them. Whether it is history, science, philosophy, psychology, finances, self-help, and so on. I promise you that the more you know, the more pieces you will put together and learn how to mold it to your life and personality in a positive way. Every book has its golden apple, that one piece of information that sticks with you going forward. I can go through my entire bookshelf and tell you one thing I learned from it and how I applied it to myself and my self-improvement. As a result, you will see your mental state strengthen dramatically and your confidence will rise to the sky motivating you to learn more once you see that knowledge pay off. Never be scared to invest in yourself, I have purchased and read countless amounts of books and will never regret a dime. Never stop learning, because knowing more than your counterpart will only put you at an advantage in every situation in life.

  In essence, to fully achieve success in these three aspects you need to constantly imagine your desired result. Making it a goal to achieve that feeling of mightiness as if you are on the top of the world needs to be a daily occurrence. Take time throughout the day to imagine your goals being achieved with those positive emotions rushing through your body, it will make you manifest it into existence. But most of all, form a plan and set up a routine so you can form new habits and discipline to achieve your goals successfully. Without a plan on how to achieve your goals, you will never get there and quit along the way. Write your goals down and explain in detail how you want to achieve them and when you would like to achieve them by. Whether you are trying to get into better shape, increase your income, or improve your mentality, having a plan and keeping track of your progress is the best way to get the results you want. Keeping track of your journey and what you have accomplished will keep you motivated and focused to stay on your path of self-growth and achieving organic confidence. Improving your health, wealth, and mentality will not happen overnight. It is something that builds over time and to be honest, it may be a frequent uphill battle for some. Just be patient and trust the process because the right things will fall in place for you even if you do not know when, it is a thing called perseverance. Confidence comes with knowledge and practice, and in time, you will see that everything in your life will start coming together smoothly, I guarantee it.

Be The Man Women Want

When it comes to dating women, there is one thing you should open your eyes to. You need to realize that we live in a society where we are raised to be the type of men women genuinely are not attracted to. The whole "Happy wife, happy life" motto is bullshit, I do not believe we have to abide by whatever the woman wants to be in a healthy and happy relationship. Men are raised to be the nice guy who is taught to do whatever she wants and how she wants it, or they are labeled as assholes or selfish men. If you truly believe that's how men are supposed to be then you need to wake up. A real woman does not want a push over or a man who is weak mentally, and a real woman sure as hell does not want a man who is easily willing to change who he is just for her without any good reason. Yet most men are raised to be that exact type of man. We are taught to be push overs, fight and beg for her even if she does not want you, and change who we are just to make her happy even if we are not. Never feel the need to be the nice guy just because you were raised to think it is the right thing to do. She might think it is adorable at first, but where is a man's positive masculinity at the end of it all? I am not telling you to mistreat her or be a misogynist, but let's face it, women get bored of men who are too nice. It not only makes them lose interest in you, but being a nice guy is not going to keep her attraction level high in the long run.

I remember one time I was on a date and the subject of relationships casually came up at dinner. She told me the last man she dated was a very successful business owner and well known locally, but she ended up calling it quits with him eventually. I asked her why even though she said the man had a good career and seemed very established, I thought it was odd she would leave him. Her response? She said the guy was *too nice*. She could not see herself sustaining any long-term interest or sexual desire because of his need to treat her like a fragile princess all the time. He would do whatever she asked from him even if it was not in his best interest to do so. She would test him to see if he had any sort of masculine backbone but folded every time by submitting thinking it was going to please her. She was the one calling the shots telling him like it is while he listened and followed. Little did he know, being too nice to a girl will eventually make you seem like a friend in her eyes, they want a man who can act like one and not a man who lets himself be overpowered. A man who can successfully keep a girl on her tippy toes is what makes her stick around or even chase you instead. Have you ever paid attention to the women who are constantly stuck on the same guy? I bet you anything he was the one who never put up with her bullshit while the rest did. Or what about the men who are considered bad boys? Women gravitate towards men like that not because they are bad people, but because bad boys never put up with nonsense. They know what they have to offer, are confident they can attract other women, and are not scared to give her the boot if she slips up one too many times. But most of all, they will always lead a woman and never put her on a pedestal as if she is above him. Bad boys carry the same attitude of abundance with women as most women do with men. They are the men that bring the porn star out of her, and nice guys are the men they give sex to only when they feel like it or when they have earned it. You do not have to be a gangster, biker, rapper, convict, jock, or anything relatable to be considered a "bad boy" like the movies portray. A bad boy is a man who see's true value in himself and never lowers his standards. A man who stands his ground and never lets himself be influenced in a negative manner and is tough mentally. Someone who is not afraid to put anyone in their place no matter who they are, especially if it is his significant other. Do not listen to women who say bad boys are horrible people, you can be a bad boy and still be a good person or partner. A lot of women tend to play the blame game saying all men are the same and we all mistreat them and cheat. Because of that stigma, we as men are expected to kiss their ass so we aren't labeled as "the same" either. Except the only thing that is "the same" is their taste in extremely toxic men, but most are not ready for that conversation just yet. Therefore, you must be strong willed and never let yourself be molded into these weak-minded men society conditions us to be from an early age. It is not what women like, so stop believing people who say otherwise.

Extra Advice:

- ✓ Always remember that your energy, words, and actions all need to positively coincide with one another. Women can feel any inadequacies in a man's persona, which is why they give you shit tests to grade your character as a man to determine if you are an alpha or a beta. As I mentioned before, women love a masculine leader who can take initiative and have the balls to not give into their bullshit. They can smell a non-confident man from a mile away, it does not take a genius to figure out you are putting up a front. She can and *will* tell the difference if it is not matching up. That usually ends with you in the friendzone or her never reaching out again. Remember you are in control of yourself, no one can get in the way of that besides you, so never second guess your abilities and always aim to better yourself in some aspect or another. Stay on your

path of self-improvement and everything will mend together effectively.
- ✓ As horrible and cliché as this sounds, it is something that I think is a good mentality to have: If you were to die tomorrow, would you be satisfied with the chances you never took? Would you be happy with the things you could have changed but never did? Would you rest in peace knowing you did everything you could in life without anything holding you back? It is a deep concept to think about, but the goal of using it is to give you the mindset that nothing can stop you from doing anything you want to do. The world is your oyster, never let anything especially when it comes to dating hold you back because of fear, you are in control of your life.

Chapter 3: Why Instagram is Better Than Using Dating Platforms

Instagram will always be my favorite social media app to find quality women. With over 1 billion active users daily, the number of women you can potentially meet is endless. Not only do a lot of people use it daily, but it is one of the most popular social media platforms out there today. Instagram's a staple choice when it comes to online dating due to the flexibility it gives you to find a variety of women to date instead of a few choices an app or website gives you to choose from. That is what makes it so valuable for online dating in general compared to dating platforms, its versatility. I will admit, there are people who have found success on dating platforms, but majority of the time that is not the case. Most are embarrassed to admit they have used one since people view it as an unnatural method to dating due to its huge reputation of being taboo and full of STD's. Yes, you might say Instagram is not one hundred percent natural either, but it is also called a social media app and not a dating app for a reason. With that being said, we all have heard of the horror stories with some of these dating apps and websites. I have stories myself and I cannot even deny that, so I will share my worst horror story with you.

    The worst experience I had was on a popular dating app. Never used one, never really thought about it either due to the reputation it had. Except a friend of mine recommended one app specifically, saying all he saw was hot women as he was swiping, nothing less. He raved on and on about the app making me want to give it a try, so I downloaded it and started swiping. After matching and briefly talking to a few, I matched with one who I thought was the best looking of them all. We started talking and chatted for a few days and eventually set up a date to have drinks that same weekend. I was brand new to the app and skeptical at first, but I decided to give this girl a shot since I felt a better vibe with her compared to the rest. Online she was great! She had a nice smile, body, and a good sense of humor so it seemed like a no-brainer to ask her out at the time since the flirtation and attraction was obvious. I felt optimistic at that point, I was looking forward to going out and meeting her since this whole dating app thing was something new for me.

Once we met everything was perfect, we were having drinks, good conversation, and the sexual tension was there one hundred percent. I was confident we were going to end the night on a great note, and I was starting to warm up to the idea of using the app more often. Except it all went downhill when she accidently lost an expensive necklace she borrowed from a friend to use that night. I tried to help her find it, but after looking for a while we unfortunately came up short and out of nowhere, she snapped. Tears immediately began falling and her persona completely changed, she began acting very aggressive telling me to "shut the fuck up" every time I said a word trying to calm her down. I was immediately turned off, being cursed out the first night you meet someone is a deal breaker. I understood her anger about losing something that was not hers, but the way she snapped was not normal and a big red flag. Therefore, I knew the date was done, so I stood up after sitting there for ten minutes in silence hearing her cry and curse and told her I would walk her out of the bar. As we are walking out, she asked if she could sit with me in my car to calm down a little before ordering her uber. I really did not want to, but I decided to play along and avoid future conflict since she was emotionally unstable and aggressive a few minutes prior. So, I said yes and proceeded walking alongside her to my car and we both got in. As we sat, she calmed down and apologized for treating me the way she did explaining why she got so upset, and her mood thankfully started turning around. I accepted her apology and told her not to dwell on it and advised her to call the bar in the morning to see if anyone turned the necklace in. Although the overall vibe was getting better, I was still over the date, and I wanted to head home as soon as possible but she kept trying to stall time. After an hour or so of talking she told me she felt great and asked if she can spend the night at my place for a good time. Even though she was calm and collected at that point, I found it very odd she invited herself over for sex when she was an aggressive, emotional wreck only an hour beforehand. That was another big red flag for me but either way, my attraction for her was gone at that point and I had a bad feeling about her regardless. I wanted to be honest, so I politely told her I would rather leave separately as friends and offered to order her an uber home. As you can guess, all hell broke loose after that. She went from flirty and happy back to emotionally unstable within seconds. She started giggling and gave me a look of pure hatred as tears began falling down her face again, and that was the moment I knew I messed up by sticking around. She then banged her fist on my dashboard looking at me and yelled, "I didn't come all the way out here to go back home! You can either take me home and have sex or you can physically drag me out of your car while I call the cops for putting your hands on me!" She even had the nerve to take her phone out and show me the dial screen while she typed 911 with her thumb over the dial button pointing to the cameras that were around the parking lot to scare me. My jaw dropped in amazement; I could not believe a woman was literally trying to blackmail me for sex.

It was crystal clear at that moment she was extremely emotionally damaged and abusive. The most disturbing part is she genuinely seemed to enjoy what was happening. The way she went back and forth from smiling and giggling saying she wanted sex to lashing out calling me a piece of shit really creeped me out. I repeatedly asked her to leave, but she refused and locked her door in pure rage with tears still falling profusely down her cheeks. I was basically stuck, each time I asked her to get out, the more hostile she became taunting me to hit her so she could have a reason to call the cops on me. She saw I was not giving in and started calling random friends telling them she was in danger so they can come and jump me, so at that point I knew this girl was not safe to be around and I got in defense mode. I had to get out of the car and call my friend so I can keep him on the phone as a witness to what was going on in case something happened, she was an absolute psychopath. I was in an empty parking lot at three o'clock in the morning being threatened and blackmailed by a girl I met off a dating app, it was unbelievable. After hours of arguing with her she eventually got tired of her "fun" as she called it and got out and I left. She took my rejection so hard that she had to find a way to make me suffer for it. Never in my life had I experienced that with a woman, I was in total shock that an attractive girl like her was capable of that. Prior to that night, I always heard stories of the crazy women others would meet off these apps, but I always thought they were exaggerating until that day when I saw it firsthand. After that incident, I gave dating platforms a break for a few months. But I was not satisfied with how the previous experience ended so I decided to be optimistic and give a different app a shot making sure I did not get myself in another situation. I knew every woman would not be that crazy and that night was partially my fault since I should have left the moment I walked her out. I ended up giving in and gave it another shot hoping for a better outcome. Although I never ran into a psycho again, every girl I met moving forward never lasted more than a date or two and never saw them again after that. I suppose that is the point with dating apps for most, so I was not necessarily surprised. Some however did end on a good note which was great, but there was something that always made me wonder why these attractive women depended on an app to find men. There was something off about most of them and that was an odd coincidence to me, and I came to realize why.

If you think about it, most attractive women have men hitting on them everywhere they go. So why would a woman need to search elsewhere such as a dating app to meet someone? Of course, there are some exceptions to that statement but if you really pay attention, you will never really see beautiful and confident women of any sort on a dating platform. If you do, they are probably fake or have an ulterior motive such as attracting business to a club or selling nudes. I realized that a lot of the women on there, not all, but most of them have major hang-ups. Some are emotionally wrecked due to their past, others are severely insecure and use it for extra validation, and the rest use it for frequent casual sex. I have a friend who once confessed he caught chlamydia three different times using dating apps! That only goes to show why these types of platforms have such a bad reputation, there is a catch that comes with most of the girls you meet. If that is not a big enough sign to avoid them, I don't know what else would be. I am not going to say Instagram eliminates potentially bad dates, because that is a possibility anywhere. The point I want to make is you can utilize Instagram to find those beautiful women you truly want without being limited by a dating platform. There is no reason to be dating women you only settle for or waking up to the sensation of lava coming out of your penis like my friend did three times. And there sure as hell is not a good enough reason to wait for a match so you can speak to a woman or be obligated to purchase features to advertise yourself to more eyes. While you make the developers rich, all you get is an ok one-night stand or women who have severe hang-ups causing unneeded issues and stress. Swiping left and right or creating profiles on multiple websites gets old, there is no substance to it. Yes, it might be a faster way to hang out with women more often, but at the end of the day you are just lowering your standards if that is all you depend on to date. Ask yourself this question: Would I rather date ten average women in a row, or five bombshells I am not scared to admit I hung out with? Raise your standards my friend! If you put the time in, you can leverage Instagram in countless ways that trump any reason to rely heavily on dating platforms again. Let's take a look and compare.

Dating Apps:

- Must buy a package or subscription for full benefits
- Less favorable options
- Limited access due to location, users, features
- Must be matched before being able to talk
- You approach the best option they give you
- Comes with the stigma of being taboo and filled with STD's

Instagram:

- Free
- Gives you more quality options to choose from
- Endless access to women

- You can speak to any mutual follower at any moment you want
- You control who you approach
- Less taboo for dating in general

The best part of all as you can see is that Instagram is totally free to use, there is no need to purchase anything to fully maximize your potential dates, everything you need to double your pipeline is right there at no cost. There are so many tactics to find your preferred type of woman, and that is without the need of swiping or spending money on extra features to meet more options. Save your money and put great faith in Instagram, it has an unlimited number of women to date, you just need to know how to find them. It may take more time, but you will undoubtedly grow your dating pipeline more organically and effectively using what I am about to teach you next.

Chapter 4: How to Maximize Your Profile for Attracting Women

We all know that majority of the time an online persona will never match your in-person persona completely due to many factors such as your personality, way of speaking, flaws, and anything else online can never truly show. Yes, you can post videos or write long captions expressing your thoughts and personality but that will never fully compare to who you are in real life. You must remember that to successfully date off social media you need to be honest with who you are and what you display. No, I am not saying to express your feelings and emotions in depth and tell your entire life story to your followers. What I am saying is give little hints to who you are and what you offer to spark curiosity. Giving those hints will spark the "who is he?" thought and make her wonder more about you leading to her actively engaging with you when you approach. Also, never act like someone you are not. If you feel the need to fake that you are rich or act like you are this untouchable stud, then you are only playing yourself. Not only do you look like an idiot but faking to be someone you are not will only attract the wrong type of people. Quality women will see it as a big red flag with the word "insecure" written on it in giant letters, so always keep that in mind. Women love a man who has a good online image and an even better one in-person, your online persona needs to translate into your physical form, always. But first, you need to set up your profile so it can reflect you and your personality as much as possible. On the following page are a few tips to consider so you can attract and sustain more female followers consistently.

Profile Picture

The first thing you must consider to even get her to click your profile or username will be your profile picture. This needs to be your best picture hands down, do not use a meme as a profile picture or leave it blank, she will automatically think you are a fake or creeping around. Use one that shows either a head shot or anything that will spark her interest or grab her attention. Your profile picture is basically the first line of bait for her to even bother seeing the rest of your profile, make sure it is the best reflection of you physically. You don't know how many times a woman has purposely found my profile picture on my page and liked it because it's what sparked their attention to click on my username in the first place. That profile picture can be the difference between her following you back or continuing to scroll down ignoring you completely.

General Pictures and Videos

When it comes to posting content, you must add variety to what you post so women will follow you. Posting pictures and videos is a good way to start, you can post anything that shows your likes and interests. If you have hobbies, a career, or certain passions like traveling or cars that can be shown off, go ahead and post it. Do not post anything blurry or extremely edited either, the more natural, the better. And always be sure to post the best picture or video of yourself that you feel confident with the way you look. You do not have to take model worthy pictures every time, but never post a picture if you have a booger showing, greasy looking hair, or food crud on your lips, that is just gross. The goal here is to be presentable, not like you live as a caveman and shower once a week.

If you have physical features you receive compliments on, use it to your advantage while posting as well. Hair, eyes, body, smile, or anything you know are your best features is always good to casually show off. You do not have to make it obvious, but letting those features be seen will make you look more attractive, because we all have our unique features that catches people's eyes. Except most of all, make sure you always mix up the way you post, using the same pose or angle every time should be avoided. It is not only boring but doing so will not make people want to follow you at all. If you want to see examples, just look at someone who is a celebrity or Instagram famous, they will always post to attract more people, it is basically their job. They are always creative with their content and snap pictures while they are out or traveling. Mirror that, experiment with different kinds of posts and when you go out, take snapshots and videos of your adventures to make you look appealing to your viewers. If you are out in a group, post with friends and other women. Posting with other people, especially other women, will show you are socially accepted, and women will see that as high value and be more attracted to you. If you do not have a big group of friends, post good pictures and snap a video of doing something sociable with other people around will work just as well, I promise. Displaying you live in a box will only push potential dates away, but showing you have an interesting life will make women curious to meet you. Especially if they see you taking pictures at the same places they go out to as well.

There are also certain characteristics of a man that sparks attraction instantly with women. One of the big ones they look at is your overall appearance. Women will judge you by the way you keep up with yourself, always. If you are posting content looking scruffy with old clothes and dirty shoes on, it is going to turn women off. Good posture, cologne if you are in public, a haircut, and being well dressed will always give you a second look by women online and in-person. You do not need to be the type that does manly pedicures and manicures and dresses in high end brands all the time. The only thing you need to do is show that you take care of yourself; a well-groomed man that smells good shows a woman you have structure in your life. If you look sloppy, they will think you are sloppy overall as well, and that is a big deal breaker for most. Posting decent content that displays you are a well-groomed man will spark attraction in women and in return they will follow you and engage with you. The posts on your profile will be the first thing a woman will see when she presses on your Instagram handle. Which is why it is best to post presentable pictures and videos of yourself, it is the first impression someone will get of you, so make it count. Evaluate yourself and find what makes you interesting and casually display it on your page so people can see your life at a glimpse. Post what *you* believe is attractive and good content, be yourself and the right women will come, the way you portray yourself will influence who you will attract. But most of all, be honest with yourself, the more you act like someone you are not the less a woman who is worth it will give you a shot. Especially if that is the impression you are giving off on your Instagram.

Captions

They give a taste of who you are mentally, they show the viewer what is on your mind and a little hint of your personality. You can keep it short and light, or you can be more expressive discussing a certain topic or passion in more depth. Either or is fine, some people like to keep it simple and some like to be more expressive, both can be used depending on the context of the post. It can be a few words, short saying, or a small paragraph to express as you please. Never be scared to express your opinion if you are speaking on something you feel strongly for such as a cause or relationship topics for example. I would also highly discourage saying anything extremely offensive or nasty just because it is within your self-interests. You can, but you will be scaring more women off than attracting them and sparking more conflict with others. Women love a man who can stand his ground with his opinions and thoughts in a mature way. If you want to write an in-depth caption, write a caption that shows a masculine mindset. Show you are a leader that speaks about interesting topics that is not afraid to speak his mind on relevant subjects and you will begin to see more women engaging on your posts ultimately sparking further conversation. Keep it all balanced and you will be on the right track!

Instagram Story

This is another great tool to use, since stories are used normally for something that is happening at the moment, post stories to make you more personable. This can be used by posting videos during a night out with friends or while doing something you want to share such as working out or anything that people would most likely engage with. The options are endless here, anything you post will give the viewers a more personalized image of you. We all know most posts that go on a story are not "page" worthy, so any little videos, memes, or pictures you have that can be used to give a more genuine view of yourself and your personality besides a pose and a snapshot is a plus. Not to mention, you can use your story to create polls, ask questions for feedback, or tag your location to garner engagement from your new or current followers. Stories are a lot of times used more than normal posts, so it is a great opportunity to open the door for good interaction since most Instagram users browse through stories just as much as normal posts on their feed.

Reels

Reels are also a good way to set your profile up, it is perfect for anyone who enjoys posting or making videos longer than the normal one-minute videos Instagram allows you to post normally. This can be a good section to post reels showing hobbies more in depth, topics you want to talk about, interesting events you were a part of, or anything along those lines that can further show you are likes and personality. It can be a great way to show versatility and expose your profile to new eyes more often since reels can trend and make your post more visible to new people on the explore page which I will explain more in depth later.

Public or Private Page

When it comes to this aspect and you want to be seen, I highly recommend leaving your profile public. Putting your page private will limit your exposure drastically especially while using the methods I am going to show you in the next chapter on building your female following. If you are concerned about your privacy, simply be selective on what you show to the public or build your following up and then set your profile to private. The good thing is you can set your profile to public or private as many times as you want within your settings.

Profile Biography

This section should be short, no need to write a novel about yourself. You can simply put a quote or tell a few things about yourself such as your occupation, age, ethnicity, etc.

Whatever you decide to write will not be a lot since Instagram limits the number of words anyways, so this is the easiest aspect of your profile to set up.

Chapter 5: How to Build Your Female Following Through Instagram

Now that we have covered how to optimize your profile to initiate a follow and attraction, let's get to the fun part on how to build your female following. There are numerous ways to do so, the methods I am going to teach you I have successfully used time and time again. The first thing I want to make clear is you need to accept the fact that not everyone will follow you back or will want to follow you either way, that is something you must get over if it bothers you. Some people care if someone does not follow them back and some do, either way do not take it too serious, Instagram is just an app at the end of the day. You also must be realistic; you cannot follow famous models only and expect them to follow you back or even respond to your messages. Why? Because you are basically just a follower to them for likes or business, you will have a better shot growing balls and approaching them in person. The women you should look for are the ones who are still beautiful but live normal lives and are not heavily dependent on social media fame. Keep in mind, you will find attention seeking women regardless of the number of followers she has, but it is a more realistic approach when getting them out on a date.

Social media does not give you that organic in-person ability to create attraction by simply having a conversation and flirting. It is all based on words in a caption, and how your persona comes off within your posts or the words used while messaging one another. You need to get a feel for the type of women who engage with your profile and posts the most, once you find your sweet spot and notice patterns on who follows you or not, you can begin to scale your following effectively and approach woman with more success. As odd and as dumb as that sounds, it is true. As you begin to post more often you will notice the types of women who engage the most and you will be able to profile certain types of females based on looks, occupation, age group, ethnicity, etc. that are most likely to fancy you. For example, I have a friend who is Caucasian, blue eyed and has blonde hair. This friend loves Latinas, but he tends to date Latinas of specific ethnicities due to a clever reason. That reason is that the men of those specific ethnicities tend to have mostly dark features meaning darker hair, eyes, and tanned skin. Since he has a lighter complexion overall, crystal blue eyes, and loves the Latino culture, the women of those ethnicities see him as different and exotic, and it attracts them. To be honest, he has been very successful with dating overall because of it. He noticed a specific type of woman gave him the most attention and maximized it. However, never take that piece of advice as your only method because that is not always the case, you can always find women of all sorts interested but you will always gain more attention from certain types of females and leveraging that will help. Some men get more attention from cougars, some women are attracted to certain ethnicities, bodybuilders usually attract women into fitness, some think a man who is into anime is sexy, and so forth. The list can go on, but that gives you multiple examples that women have their preferred type of man, and that type may just be you. The same rule of thumb can be applied when you are out at a bar or club trying to meet women. The best chances of picking up a woman will always be the one who is making eye contact on multiple occasions and has some sort of body language showing she is trying to get your attention. It is the golden sign of interest while in person and profiling a type of woman on Instagram who is more likely to fancy you can be taken in the same context.

As I mentioned before, Instagram is the most effective social media platform since it is a lot less family oriented than other platforms and a lot more direct to connect with a woman. You can have ten thousand followers and most of them can be women, you are not limited to how many people can follow you like other social media platforms. Not only that, but you are not obligated to follow everyone back as well, so it is a lot more controllable in all aspects making it that much more personalized. Most of the men who ask me where I find all these women always say they have no idea where to look, and it is honestly right there. Many have not looked around enough to fully explore what Instagram has to offer. It may take more time than a simple swipe or match, but I promise you the results will be worthwhile. Here are my top five methods on how to build your female following.

Post Often

To start, you need to post often, whether it is on your main page, story, or reels. Instagram has an algorithm; they want people to be consistently active using the app at all angles. When it comes to your posts being seen, some of your followers may not even see your posts at all and some will see every single one. The rule to abide by is the more you post, the more Instagram will recognize you are active and will put your content at the top of more of your followers' feeds. Not only will this boost your posts to the top of your followers' feeds but posting often can also land your posts on the explore page. The explore page has the potential to expose your content to hundreds, if not thousands of new eyes potentially giving you more followers without any effort. It is also recommended to interact with the people you follow or your general followers as well. Interacting with other users such as liking their posts back or responding to messages or comments gives your posts a higher chance of being pushed to the top of their feeds every time you post. You do not have to post every day, well you can, but it all depends on your preferences. Anywhere from three to four times a week is good, or every few days would work just as well. Some people post more on their stories, some only post on their page, but I would highly recommend using all angles Instagram gives you to get your posts in front of more and more eyes, especially women. The more active you are, the better it will be to gain new followers and interact with your current followers.

If you are not familiar with what the *Explore Page* is; it is the section where Instagram shows you trending posts based on the kind of content you actively engage with. For instance, if you are big into sports and follow a lot of professional athletes and teams, the explore page will be full of posts related to sports and other athletes as well. The explore page will not only display what Instagram thinks you will like, but it also allows you to browse through different users, hashtags, and locations. If you are confused on where it is located, it is at the bottom of the screen with the magnifying glass as the icon right next to the home button.

Current Male or Female Followers

Your current female followers that live locally can easily be leveraged to find women within your area. We all know women are very interactive with one another especially on social media, so most of the women they follow who are not celebrities or instafamous models are usually friends or people who live locally as well. All you need to do is go to her profile and browse through who she is following or follows her, and you will find plenty of profiles to browse through allowing you to add as you please. On the flip side, the same process can be used with your male followers also. Whether it is a friend, acquaintance, or anyone you know with a public profile can be used to find women as well. They most likely will follow and be followed by local women so you can use the same exact method and accomplish the same amount of success. Both ways are great hands-on tactics to find a lot of local women for you to follow and connect with in the future. Yes, you may think that is slightly stalker-like, but I guarantee you are not the only one doing it, there are no written rules stating you cannot do so. I have had friends tell me they go on other people's profiles or the pages of male models to add tons of women, doing so is not going to be something new so never be scared to try it. Social media was made for you to connect with others, there is no right or wrong way to connect with other users when you see people going to the extent of paying to advertise their page for exposure. This is simply another way to do it for free and will probably be one of the easiest ways to build your pipeline.

#Hashtags

Method 1:

Hashtags should be a staple in every post you upload on Instagram, because they can be used in numerous ways. When posting, I recommend using anywhere from five to ten hashtags, you can place it directly under your caption or comment the hashtags in the comments section no longer than 1 minute after posting if you prefer the caption to be clean. The more hashtags you use the more spammy it looks, keep that as a rule of thumb when using them but never use less than five hashtags. The reason you need to use hashtags to grow your following is because it places your post under a hashtag page, so if anyone uses the same hashtag and visits that specific hashtag page, it will display your post to hundreds of eyes immediately. Some very common hashtags such has #love, #summer, #peace or anything along those lines can have millions if not over a billion posts listed under it. Keep in mind that using very common hashtags can make your post buried quick due to the thousands of people using it daily, so use ones that have less action as well to mix it up to give your posts better chances of being viewed longer. If you are looking to expose your post to female eyes specifically, use any subtle hashtags that you know a woman would most likely visit or use on their own posts. Some examples would be #fashion, #relationshipgoals, #beauty, #success, #confidence, or anything along those lines will work. If you do not know what to use, just google "trending hashtags" and a ton of websites will pop up immediately for you to reference.

Another way that is beneficial would be relating your hashtags to your caption, what you are doing, wearing, or place you may have been at the time whether it is a restaurant, nightlife location, or city that are more specific and less saturated. If your caption is about positivity for example, use hashtags related to positivity or the message you are trying to pass on. If you are wearing a nice outfit with name brands, relate your hashtags to those brands or general fashion. If the post was at a local bar or restaurant, use hashtags related to that location, setting, or cuisine. There are endless ways to utilize hashtags that will positively expose your post to the right audience. Choosing not to use hashtags on your post will make it visible only to whoever follows you. It is a great tool to get yourself seen by new women and everyone else on Instagram potentially gaining more followers at the same time.

Method 2:

The second way to use them is by browsing specific hashtags and viewing the posts listed within that page. You will see plenty of women's posts right there front and center. If you want to find women who use hashtags of your city, simply press the long search bar section at the top of the explore page. Then, once you see the drop down directly under the search bar containing tabs that say "Top, Accounts, Tags, Places," press the tab that says "Tags" and search the city you are looking for. Once you search the specific city, you will find a variety of hashtags listed containing the city name and the number of posts that have been posted under that specific hashtag for you to browse. Now, press on the hashtag page that sparks your interest and you will be able to browse as many posts as you want at your own leisure.

After that, all you need to do is click on the profiles of women you find attractive and begin engaging with them. This can be done by liking a few posts to spark their attention or by simply following them. The good thing is you can search any hashtag you want, whether it is the name of a city, park, hangout spot like a club or bar that is popular, and so forth giving you the ability to find posts of local people. Hashtags are ultimately the quickest vessel between users, you can even directly follow hashtag pages on Instagram as if you are following an actual person's account. Meaning any new posts that are tagged under that hashtags page can show up directly onto your feed, all you do is hit the follow button at the top of that hashtags page. It will immediately connect you with others who share your common interests and thoughts, use it to your advantage.

Location

Location is one of the best back-door methods to find local women in your area, and it is honestly my preferred method if you want to connect with local women as soon as possible. The best way to start is to add your location to your posts, this is done in the same section where you write your caption and edit your photos before posting content. Within that section, you will see a tab directly underneath the caption area that says, "Add Location" and from there you can search any location and tag it on the post. Tagging your location is a great tactic to use, the best thing about it is you can choose any location to tag, it is not limited to your physical location at that moment. Once you add your location upon uploading, your post will be listed within that locations page (like the hashtag pages) along with everyone else who tagged the same location as well. That is a great way to show your followers that you are local, and many women prefer to follow local men, so it is important they know you are close by. Or even better, other women can find you if they happen to be browsing that locations page and see your post, potentially following you as a result.

Not only that, but you can use the same exact process with hashtag pages and browse the location's page itself whether it is a general geographical area or an actual physical location. It allows you to find women who are located within your area or go to the same places you do, and it is an amazing method to build your local following. It works the same as searching for hashtags, press the long search bar at the top of the explore page and on the drop-down press on the "places" tab instead, and from there search any location or place you prefer. For example, if you search the name of your gym, you can browse your gym's location page and see the women tagging your gyms location on their posts. It is a great way to add them directly and a great ice breaker to use if you happen to run into them while working out, she will already recognize you from Instagram. It also works great when you are searching for the location of local bars, clubs, universities, restaurants, towns, cities, or anywhere that is an active spot that people would tag their posts with. You will see plenty of women posting pictures with their friends at that same club, bar, school, or wherever the place may be. It is an incredibly reliable way to find and connect with numerous amounts of local females and build your following at the same time. Whether you search your general city's location or dig deeper into specific places within your area, you will undoubtedly find great local women to follow and potentially date. It will be the easiest way to successfully see what your city or town has to offer!

Nightlife Profile Pages, Local DJs, and Local Promoters

The last method to source quality women is visiting local nightlife profile pages. This can be a bar, lounge, club, or even a restaurant that turns into a club at night. Mostly every single nightlife spot has its own Instagram page to advertise their events and specials for that upcoming night or weekend. This is an awesome way to connect with new people because women are not likely to follow a club or bar's page if they are not local to that area. Use the same exact process with hashtag and location pages but instead, search under the "accounts" tab on the drop-down bar. Once you find a specific club or bars profile page, browse who follows them and start engaging. You will see that most of their followers are all women for obvious reasons. All nightlife businesses have ladies' night events and drink specials to attract more female attendees, women will follow these pages so they can stay in the loop for their next girls' night out.

The other way to do this is to follow your local club promoters or DJs on Instagram or visit their page if their profile is public. The local club promoters and DJs in your area that promote various events at clubs or bars will have local women following them for the same exact reasons. Club promoters and DJs are always posting about the next upcoming event or weekly party and the drink specials they will have available, which are mostly catered to women. You already know local women will follow them for updates and free entry hookups for paid events. If you do not know where to find a local club promoter or DJ on Instagram, they can normally be found by looking through a club or bars location page or by going directly to their Instagram profile and looking at their tagged photos. Tagged photos can be found by pressing the tab with a square icon of a head and torso located right below the biography section on their profile, you cannot miss it. Most promoters and DJs will tag the location and the Instagram profile of the club or bar directly on the photo when posting their promotion flyer for an upcoming event. Use both methods to your advantage if you visit a certain place often or just browse all the nightlife profile pages within your area. You will see loads of local women to follow, growing your pipeline successfully.

Extra Advice:

- ✓ Be sure to use all these methods interchangeably to get the best results. You need to keep in mind that some hashtags or locations do not get much traffic especially if it is an uncommon hashtag or location that not too many people go to. That is when you explore more options within your area or use the other methods listed above for better results. Using all of them consistently will be the best way to effectively find women and build your female following.

CAUTION:

Be aware that Instagram has an algorithm that tracks spam accounts. If you like too many posts or follow too many people within a 24-hour period, they will action block you. Being action blocked means that Instagram is punishing you for violating their community guidelines. The Instagram algorithm basically picks up on spam-like activities and will temporarily block you from following, unfollowing, liking, or even commenting on posts if you exceed the daily limit within their guidelines. Many people were creating bots that would automatically like, comment, and follow people on a mass level and they started cracking down on it. So, for following and unfollowing do not exceed more than 200 actions a day. As for liking, keep it under 600 likes per day to prevent getting action blocked. Although many of you will not exceed that limit in a day, it is always good to know just in case. Action blocks can last a few hours up to weeks if it gets bad enough, so always be weary of spending hours adding and liking pictures to attract more followers, it will add up fast.

How to Engage to Get Yourself Noticed

If you add a someone and they follow you back, you do not necessarily need to engage to get yourself noticed since she already acknowledged you. Wait for new and better opportunities to engage or take action. But if you sent a request or followed her public profile and did not get a follow back, there are ways to get noticed. First thing I would recommend is liking numerous posts of hers so when she opens her feed, the odds of her noticing you will be much higher. Doing so will spark her curiosity to see who you are and visit your profile, it works every time, trust me. If you only like one post, you are not going to be noticed especially if she recently posted a picture and the likes are pouring in. Be sure to engage appropriately, if she has hundreds of posts and you try to like every single one, that is going to make you look like a stalker so please avoid that at all costs. I would engage on three to seven posts; like her most recent posts and a few that were posted prior because engaging on an older post will show you are paying attention and not liking just because. However, if you want to comment, comment on maybe one or two posts at the most and that is it. When you do, comment something relevant to what her caption states or something you like about the post. Never comment anything portraying you are drooling over her, the goal here is to catch her attention, not show you are desperate for a follow back. You can give her a light compliment on her outfit or agree/disagree with a point she is trying to make within her caption, keep it simple. If you engage correctly and she ends up following you, the odds of her responding will be higher when the time to approach comes since you will already be a familiar face. These tactics can also be used if you want to bait someone to follow you as well. If you come across a woman's profile that is public but prefer not to follow her first, you can engage on her posts to see if she follows you or shows engagement back. If she does either or, it will give you the green light to follow because the chances of her following back are high.

But remember what I am about to tell you, and this is speaking in general for when you already initially engaged, and you have followed each other for a while. *Do not* show too much engagement or she will see you as a just a follower, not a person of potential interest. There are too many men that like or comment on every single post making them look desperate thinking it is the best way to get the attention of a woman. Doing that will make her accustomed to your engagement putting her on an even higher pedestal, feeding into her need of social media validation. If you have spoken already and have built good repour and she engages the same way back, that is fine and a lot more acceptable. But the best thing is to keep your comments minimal and likes enough to at least demonstrate you interact with her posts and show her love. Never make yourself look like a fan, women laugh at the guy sending ten messages at a time or posting comment after comment drooling over their posts. They will see you with pity rather than respect, a needy beta rather than a grounded alpha. So, believe me, if you hold back on your engagement, she will notice you more when you do. All women check who has liked their pictures and who has commented on their posts. She will notice you do not validate every single post and see your engagement as if she did something right, especially if she has interest in you. Never forget, a woman handles the attention she gets online similarly to the attention she gets in person. She will take the validation from the guy who does not show he is desperate a lot more seriously than the validation of the guy who never leaves her alone.

Weeding Out Fake Profiles

We all have those suspicious profiles that are a little fishy, here are a few ways to tell if a profile is fake.

Followers to Following Ratio

Many catfish profiles have a very low number of followers and follow a ton of people. If a woman is extremely beautiful and her profile is public with only 50 followers, but she is following 900 others, something is off since we all know most women who are very attractive naturally have hundreds or thousands of followers. Keep that in mind when coming across profiles in which their followers to following ratio is off, most women will always have way more followers than people they follow back. On the contrary, I have met women whose followers to following ratio is off, but they were real. This rule usually pertains to the profiles that seem too good to be true with the woman looking like a supermodel or a porn star.

Tagged Friends

Another good indicator is if they have any tagged friends in their pictures. If they have lots of pictures with other people but no one is tagged, that is a red flag to take into consideration. As stated before, women are social people, they love taking pictures and tagging their friends when they post. So, if she has a bunch of posts with friends and none are tagged, it could mean it is a fake profile. Keep an eye out for that.

Tagged Pictures

As mentioned above, women are social, so looking into their tagged photos by others is another great way to weed out catfish profiles. If you don't see any pictures tagged or the tagged pictures are of random spam posts, then that's a concern to have. Most of the time you will see tagged pictures of them with friends and family whether it's recent or from the past.

Reverse Image Search

This would be a last resort to use, I would only recommend this if you are interested in a woman on a more serious level but have your doubts. This is done when you take a picture and reverse search it on google or other downloadable apps that do the same function. All you do is screen shot the picture, crop it, and upload it to see if the website or app can find the same picture elsewhere on the internet. This way is slightly harder because it usually never yields good results, I have caught fake profiles before using this method but only a handful of times. It is not common to get direct matches at first on a photo you reverse search, you will most likely have to search multiple to get a hit. This method normally works best with women who seem too good to be true such as supermodels and women who look like porn stars as well.

Chapter 6: The Approach

Now that you have learned how and where to find women on Instagram, it is time to start planning your point of approach. Some women do not openly display the relationships they are in, and some do not even bother opening messages due to the amount they get, so never take a woman who does not respond to heart every time. Some girls refuse to use social media to date period, so keep increasing your female following and you will find a bunch who are open to it. Dating is a numbers game, the more women you approach, the faster and more effective your pipeline will grow. Many men go to bars and clubs and talk to multiple women before they land one who is interested giving them a real opportunity. The more women you approach, the more women you will be able to take out and date. You do not have to message twenty new women a day either, just keep a good pace on the number you do approach, and the results will come.

    One point I would like to address is the fact that many men believe it is necessary to always have super corny pick-up lines to get a female's attention online or in-person. Remember, every woman is different! Yes, some do love cornball lines, and then some think it is really weird and prefer a simple introduction. Other women get bothered when you ask too many questions thinking you are interviewing them, and some like it because they see you are interested in getting to know her. Some love aggressive and forward men and some like men who are respectful and courteous until she gets comfortable with you. Also, by aggressive I mean being upfront with your intentions and actions, not by sending dick pics or multiple messages a day saying you want her sexually. Women do not react well to being sexualized at first, that is the worst way to approach and the best way to get blocked and put on blast for all her friends to see. Each woman has her own likes and dislikes when it comes to being approached by men. A lot of women get attention constantly, and it all boils down to whether she wants to talk or how long you can keep her engaged in conversation to spark real interest. My best advice is to approach her online the same way you would in person, it should never be made more complicated than that. Be yourself, but approach with confidence and fearlessness. No matter what you say or do, if she has high enough interest in you, she will respond and engage in conversation. Saying the wrong thing or making a wrong move turning her off making her cut communication is a whole other conversation, but if a woman has high interest, she will respond and keep engaging. But, before I get into the different ways to approach, let's compare and contrast an online approach with an in-person approach. Each approach is self-explanatory, one is face to face and the other is not, but let's take a look and evaluate a little more.

Online Approach

Pros:

- Faster form of contact
- Less approach anxiety
- Endless options
- Saves money (No need to offer a drink or food)
- Doubles your dating pipeline faster
- Makes rejection lighter and easier to learn from at first
- You are in control of who you want to approach each time

Cons:

- Cannot read body language, attitude, or red flags easily
- Approach anxiety is still a possibility
- Too many options can be overwhelming at times
- Money can still be wasted if you meet, and the date goes sour
- Profiles may be fake
- Rejection is still unavoidable
- People can look different in pictures than they do in person

In-Person Approach

Pros:

- It gives you a better feel for a person's energy
- Eliminates the chance of getting catfished
- Easier to seduce and flirt during conversation
- You are in control of who you approach in-person
- Forms emotional and physical connections faster
- Keeps face-to-face communications skills in check
- You can control interactions better and form attraction easier

Cons:

- Slower form of contact
- Higher chance of approach anxiety
- Limited options due to location or place
- Rejection can sting more in-person
- Takes more time, effort, and potential spending
- Slower pipeline growth

As you can see, each approach has its debatable pros and cons based on comparisons. Except an in-person approach needs to be equally as strong or even stronger than your online approach. Without a strong in-person approach you will never feel truly comfortable with online approaching. You need to have a strong natural base, or you will run into communication difficulties once you get a woman out on a date wondering what to do next. Or even more, you can coincidentally run into someone of interest in public who you have spoken to online and that is where you need to take initiative and approach her in person. They both need to be strong, and you need to be just as confident with each method or it will be difficult to leverage the positive aspects of both approaches. Yes, online approaching brings less stress and more results, but take the positives and negatives from both approaches and use it to your advantage, do not let anything hinder you from a potential great date or relationship. Now, let's begin with the ways to approach, there is the direct approach and the indirect approach, each can be successful, but it is up to you to decide which one fits best.

Direct Approach

A direct approach is when you let a woman know you have high interest in her immediately from the start. This is done by approaching her with a direct flirtatious line or any other action that indicates you are interested in her. There are numerous ways that a direct approach can be done, so it is up to you on which one you think fits your personality better. Bear in mind, to do this effectively it must be done with total confidence, or she will sense the insecurity in your words and actions. Also, there is no need to be overly sexual or creepy especially if it is your first attempt of contact, being slightly flirtatious is totally fine. The point here is to initiate conversation and show her you are into her without being too pushy. Here are a few lines that you may take into consideration when direct approaching, these are a few of many that can be used.

- "You're absolutely gorgeous, I couldn't help but introduce myself, my name is (your name). What's yours?"

- "I don't mean to be forward but, you look like someone I'd love to meet (insert flirtatious emoji) What's your name?"

- "Everything about you is my type of woman. I have to ask, are you single?"

As I mentioned before, there is no wrong way to do a direct approach since you are letting her know you are interested from the start. Direct approach lines work best with women who like assertive men or have shown clear signs of interest on their end. This is the best way to show you are forward and direct, and many women love that. If you are not being rude, disrespectful, or saying anything way out of line, you are in the clear either way. Many men overthink on what lines to use, but it all comes down to whether she has interest in you or not in the first place to entertain the approach. A man she is not attracted to can use a cringeworthy pickup line and she will be quick to call him a weirdo, but a man she thinks is sexy can say the same thing and will laugh it off thinking it was cute. It is not always the words one uses that catches her attention, but the simple fact that she is attracted to you as well. Not to say words are not important because that is how you communicate and connect on an emotional level to build more attraction, that is a huge part of it too. But when you first meet someone, physical attraction is a key player to even get to that point, especially when it is online. When you want to directly approach a woman, send her a direct message or respond to her post or story and lay it on her.

Extra Advice:

- ✓ There will be times when women will be bold and start blowing up your feed with likes and comments or interact with your stories often. That is a great signal to approach her at any time since that is a strong sign of interest. If you want to keep her on her toes, show her love back and wait a little before sending the first message to keep her anticipating your approach.
- ✓ If she gives you obvious signals, you do not have to ask her out immediately or tell her you are interested in her right then and there. The simple fact of reaching out to spark a conversation is one hundred percent ok as well. The lines listed above are more for cold approaching when you see a woman you like and want to be assertive.
- ✓ When you do send her the first message, wait a few hours up to one full day to respond. This will show her you are a man with priorities and are not desperate for her conversation. They may not tell you directly, but that tactic will have the question "How come he took so long to respond back?" stuck in their head when every other guy responded immediately. That is a turn off to a lot of women when men have nothing better to do than respond within seconds. Except do not take too long to respond, the point is to keep her on her toes, not waiting until she loses interest.
- ✓ Be smart with who you send messages to if you approach multiple women consistently. Keep in mind that a lot of women know each other whether it

is through social media or personally if you are targeting them in your local area. Try to avoid sending loads of messages to women you see are friends or have many mutual followers. The reason I say that is because women communicate with one another, and if you try to talk to a whole circle of friends and use the same exact lines or techniques to hit on them, they *will* find out. If you do not care, be sure you are on point with your game because if it is weak, best believe they will laugh about it and a man with weak game spreads through the grape vine fast.

Indirect Approach

An indirect approach is when you avoid displaying high levels of interest from the start, you spark friendly conversation first before directly showing your interest. This can be viewed as a vetting process by testing the waters and dropping hints of attraction to see if she shows any signs of interest on her end before asking her out. This approach can go either two ways; she fully engages showing signs of interest too, or eventually it dies off because the interaction was strung on for way too long never getting past a friendly level. This approach can be tricky, only because if you wait too long before showing any sort of real interest, she may friendzone you or think you do not see her in a romantic sense. As you begin to talk to numerous women, you will learn how to feel conversations out and sense where they are going so you can move forward accordingly. I have done indirect approaches with multiple women and have dealt with them differently. I may indirectly approach someone and within hours have her number, and another I may need more time to feel her out on different occasions with small talk until I see it is worth pursuing further. Both have ended in successful dates, so it is something you do at your own comfort level as you learn how to feel the vibe of the given situation. It will be something you will feel naturally, so always go with your gut instinct and never second guess yourself. Here are the two best ways to indirect approach.

Reply her story

Since most people post on their story more than their actual page, it is the perfect tool to use if you want to indirectly approach her and spark conversation. Most women love to display what they are doing throughout the day whether it is what they are eating or the typical "should I buy these jeans?" question even though she's obviously trying to show off her ass. It gives you a lot of bait to use to connect with her on anything you have a mutual interest on. Maybe she is at a local bar you visit often, or she posts a story of her watching a movie you just saw too and use that as leverage to start talking and then transition to other topics. There are countless amounts of ways to do so and taking advantage of every opportunity will help you start talking to numerous women consistently. From there, you can have better judgement on her interest level with you.

If you are a little confused on how to do a successful indirect approach, I will share an example. One time, I was casually browsing through some Instagram stories when I saw one of someone posting a video of sushi. I am an avid sushi lover, and the girl who posted happened to be someone I had my eye on for a while at the time. She videoed herself expressing how amazing her go-to sushi spot is showing off her rolls. I saw that as the perfect opportunity to indirectly approach her, so I used our common love for sushi to my advantage. With that being said, I commented stating how her sushi made me want to go to my favorite spot as well and I thanked her for making me crave it in a teasing manner. As a response, she laughed and teased back telling me her spot was better than mine and from there, the conversation took off. It eventually led to other topics which then led to a sushi date a week later at my spot, and let's just say it became her favorite spot too after that night. So, as you can see, something as simple as that can be a smooth transition from an indirect approach to a date in a matter of a week. The point is to not make it obvious you are trying to hit on her at first. If she had not given me positive feedback to my response on her story or ignored it, I would have known her interest was not there all the way.

Reply to her post

This is another great alternative if she has not posted anything on her story and uploads normal content to her page. When she uploads a new post, press the "Direct Message" icon that looks like an arrow pointing to the upper right-hand corner and send a message right away to her inbox. Be careful, because when you press that icon, you will need to search their username and select it to make sure the message is being delivered to them directly, not someone else by accident. If you double check before sending, you will avoid sending it to the wrong person. But indirectly approaching this way will allow you to send her a direct message replying to the post without the need of leaving an open comment or random message if you want to be more subtle to spark a conversation. It is a rather illusive way to sneak in an ice breaker and can be used in the same context as replying to her story.

Extra Advice:

- ✓ Whether you are replying to her story or post, make sure it is something relevant to what she is posting. Keep it as authentic as possible, using any little reason to approach her indirectly can easily backfire on you. It is easy to tell you are not being sincere or coming up with random things to get her attention, that will make you look too shy and insecure. Approach her with something you can relate to or carry a conversation about before branching off onto other topics.

✓ Replying on her story or post is a good opportunity to say a joke or something smart to get her more engaged. Since most women love to show off their daily activities, they will tend to let loose more often and post something funny or act goofy in their story and that will be a great chance to use a little humor. No woman likes a guy with a dry personality, show some humor whenever the right opportunity comes.

Categorizing Women

Before we get into the conversation chapter, there is one thing I think every single man should do while talking to any woman. You need to have the ability to categorize the women you are speaking to whether it is in person or text. By categorizing I do not mean by class, race, or level of interest, what I mean by that is categorizing her as submissive or dominant. No, I am not referring to the 50 Shades of Grey type of thing, I am referring to their personality. Why is it important to know this now before we get into the conversation chapter? Because evaluating what category she falls into will give you the ability to know what to expect from her character. Many men fail to tell the difference and handle each woman the same exact way and wonder why their actions or tactics do not work on every girl. It is because dominant and submissive women have two completely ways of handling relationships and what they expect from men. Knowing the difference can not only help you know how to handle them, but it can save you from wasting time if one type or the other turns you off. Although this is something that will be easier to distinguish in person, it still applies to text conversations and is equally important. Some will give clues via text whether they are submissive or dominant just by the things they say and how they act. Make sure to pay attention as much as you can, it will help your game with women at all angles once you master how to tell them apart. So, here is a breakdown of what to expect from each side and how to handle it.

Dominant Women

I will go over two types, a woman who is truly dominant, and a woman who is dominant but can submit. Firstly, I will go over a truly dominant woman. A truly dominant woman likes to take control of situations, is bossy, and is normally the one who calls the shots romantically and financially. Most are set in their ways and will target submissive men to better fit their dominant nature. They want the power and normally date emotionally weak men since weaker men are more likely to submit compared to strong-willed men. Their overall goal is to mold the man to how they want him to be. Just look at any of your friends who get bossed around and praise the "happy wife, happy life" motto, I bet their significant other is a truly dominant woman. Men like that shape their entire life around what their girlfriend or wife wants in fear of her reaction if he does not comply. Except one key thing to know is some can show their dominance overtly or covertly depending on their personality.

Overt Dominance:

- She will make specific demands and guidelines for you to follow

- She will directly threaten to take away sex or break-up if you fail her expectations
- She will want to make the final decision and disregard your input
- She will request that you ask for her permission on certain things (personal space, spending, nights out with friends)
- She will set boyfriend duties (hold her bags, open her doors, pull her chair out)
- She will dictate when to give you sex and how she will give it

Covert Dominance:

- She will act loving and supportive when you give her what she wants but psychologically invalidate you when you do not
- She will use kisses, sex, and praise the moment you comply to her demands as a reward
- She will innocently try persuading you to agree with her opinions, outlooks, and decisions
- She will use manipulative psychology such as playing the victim and the blame game to make you feel responsible

Those are a few generalized key points, but overall, truly dominant women want to be the alpha whether they show it directly or not. If you want me to be honest, being a man with alpha tendencies who likes to lead does not mesh well with a woman who is truly dominant long term. Something temporary can work but if it is on a serious level heads will constantly clash. While you try to lead, the overtly dominant ones shut you down always challenging your actions and decisions. And the covertly dominant ones will always play the victim or try to use manipulation to get what she wants until she receives it or snaps when she does not. If you do run into this type, the best way to handle them is by never breaking your masculine frame no matter what. They will either leave with a level of respect towards you or they will never take it past a casual level. Being an alpha will turn any woman on, even a truly dominant one, which can lead to casual sex or a temporary fling, but I would not expect it to go past that level unless she submits. A lot of men submit and think it is the best card to play but that just leads to her seeing you as a beta telling all her friends how much bullshit you deal with just for some sex. Being bold and strong is what makes a woman talk about you with respect leading to other women becoming curious on getting to know you too.

Also, if you are just getting to know her, it is less likely she will show her dominance until she gets more comfortable and slips up. In the meantime, as you date and have some fun, they will show little signs in-between as you get more acquainted which will help you distinguish her true nature. I have dated truly dominant women casually and have had great times with them, but once I notice the cues indicating her dominance, I shut it down or move on. Which is why paying attention to the signs are important. If she is making final decisions without your input, requesting apologies for simple things, or is always trying to control the interaction while out of a date will be a few major signs to consider. So, if you see any signs, never obey what she wants you to do just because she wants it that way specifically without any logical reason. Especially if you do not agree with what she is requesting or asking from you. If you allow something, it is because you see she has a logical reason behind it. Not because she demands it or tells you she will perform a sexual act if you give in. To be clear, that does not mean saying no to every little thing because you think she is trying to dominate you; it means always keeping your masculine frame strong and never obeying what she wants just because she wants it that way. It is one thing if she says she wants to stop at her favorite bar for a drink before heading to the main location on a date but wanting to change everything you planned just because is another. Fighting her on everything will only led to arguments, trust me because I have done it. Keep a level head and play the game with her but never let her overpower you. Submitting yourself completely to a dominant woman will make her see you as a toy to play around with, giving you zero respect. Constantly testing your boundaries to see how far she can take it until she gets bored and moves on or settles because she knows you will follow and comply. Dating a truly dominant women will always be an uphill battle for an alpha unless you fully submit and allow yourself to be the bitch of the relationship. If not, you will always be in a disagreement on who runs the show because most of them cannot change how they are. It is a huge blow to their ego when they cannot have the power which is why they tend to use force or aggression once they see they cannot obtain it cordially.

The only way it will work out long term is if you meet a dominant woman who can submit. They are the ones who are dominant but will submit *only* if the man is doing things right. If you cannot act like a man, she will never treat you like one and step all over you. That is why your masculine frame is so important, keeping your alpha tendencies sharp will always be the best way to handle dominant women period. The ones who submit generally have natural leadership characteristics but still expect the man to be the captain at the end of the day. They will act like an alpha until the right man comes along to change their stance. That is the key difference between a truly dominant woman and one who will allow themselves to submit. While truly dominant women scrutinize you for being an alpha, women who are dominant but also grounded mentally will let you take the reins once she can trust you as her leader. Yes, she may test you to measure your stance as a man but that is their natural feminine nature. It is the same thing when men measure how much value a woman can bring as a potential wife, that is our own version of doing the exact same thing. The day she realizes you can stand your own as a man and lead, is the day she will submit. But the day you lead and get scrutinized for it, is the day you know she is set in her ways and not worth your time. Being an alpha will always be the correct play with all dominant women, because the truly dominant ones will be weeded out as time goes along.

Submissive Women

Submissive women, including dominant women who can submit, expect the man to lead and take initiative always whether it is in the bedroom, on dates, or any situation that fits. Submissive women are an alpha's sweet spot because everything an alpha does is what submissive women expect from a man. They respect masculinity; they love a man who can take charge, make them feel protected, and is not afraid to take control. Not a boy who allows himself to be pushed around, is lazy, or cries on her shoulder every time he gets a booboo on his finger. They do not like weak men, because weak men let the woman take control and a woman wo submits expects to be led. No matter how attractive you are to her, she will lose interest and move on to the next man who shows his true masculine nature if you do not. Not to say a submissive woman cannot take charge, but they find it extremely sexy when the man does instead. They give value to your opinion and will ask for your advice or expect you to make the final decision or judgement. You can notice if a woman is submissive just by the way she answers or reacts to your questions, suggestions, and decisions. They will most likely go with the flow on most things you say or the decisions you make. They will trust your judgement without the urge of trying to change it unless there is a valid reason. She will respect you, expecting you to play the role of the leader, protector, and the seducer all at once. It is what turns them on the most, that feeling of being able to count on you. They are easier to deal with because unlike truly dominant women, they will not try to control or mold you into someone that fits their dating preference. She sees you as her king and herself as your queen, not her as the queen and you as her jester. A submissive woman tends to embrace masculine energy, while truly dominant women try to belittle it. They will not threaten you, form a scene, or sweet talk your ear off to get their way. In their eyes a man should lead, and if he does not, then he is not a true man, and they move on.

The only drawback with submissive women is many can carry baggage from past relationships due to their passive nature. Many men who are truly dominant themselves will mistreat submissive women causing emotional damage and trust issues, which is unfortunate. Some women will know how to move past their experiences, but some will carry that baggage over to you. Making them act clingy or suspicious of everything you do since they have gone through a lot in their previous relationships. So, the best thing to do is address their actions in a mature manner. Tell them directly why their actions bother you and that you prefer not to tolerate it long-term. Especially if you never gave them a solid reason to act that way or barely know each other to begin with. Not all will act like this, but as you date more, the ones who do will come around sooner or later. The best way to handle a submissive woman overall is simple, be an alpha. Take initiative always, whether you are planning a date, making a move on her, or taking action when a situation arises. Take the reins and be assertive, show her what positive masculinity is all about. Remember, being a narcissist or controlling is *not* being an alpha, that is being insecure and a shitty person. Being overbearing, jealous, and controlling over a woman is not the right way to show your masculinity. That only causes toxic relationships and puts you in the same category as a manipulative and dominant woman. All they are looking for is a man. Never be afraid or too shy to show it because a man who cannot take proper action is one of the biggest turn-offs for women in general.

Extra Advice:

- ✓ You can meet hundreds of dominant and submissive women, but not every single one will be the same as the other. Some women are affectionate, jealous, or emotional, and some may be distant, indifferent, or dry and still be considered dominant or submissive at the same time. It all has to do with their personality and how they handle relationships, that is what truly categorizes them as dominant or submissive in general. You must adapt as you go, the definitions I gave above are generalities. Pay attention as you get to know one another online and when you meet in person, it will help you know what to expect and how to go about different situations.

Chapter 7: The Conversation

You are up to speed on where to find women and how to approach them, now it is time for the actual conversation. The conversation is the most crucial part to get a woman fully invested and interested. As I mentioned before, some get messages often, so you must know how to carry on a good conversation to keep her interest high and consistent until you eventually meet. One thing you need to understand is that talking online is not a face-to-face interaction, things can be easily misconstrued or taken a different way easily. Which means you must be careful with what you say and how you say it, or it can lead to arguments and her going ghost. In this chapter I will go over how to qualify a woman via text, how to flirt, show confidence, and how to keep the conversation going during this stage with a woman. I will show you some good tips and tricks to make a conversation a success whether it is through direct message, regular text message, or even in-person when you get her out on a date if it applies.

Timing

Timing is an important factor when messaging. As I mentioned during the approach chapter, it is always recommended to take some time before answering her after your first attempt of contact. She will not only be curious on why you took so long, but she will see you with a little more respect as a result. I can assure you every other guy responds within seconds like he has nothing better to do, that is a direct sign of desperation. Once she replies and you take your grace period to send another message back, you need to read her texting pace immediately. She will either take time in-between her responses or she will be consistent and have a flowing conversation, so you need to mirror whatever her pace is to an extent. Never mirror her response times exactly, she will notice a pattern making you look predictable so please avoid that. If she responds around every hour, respond back within forty-five minutes to an hour and a half later to keep the pace similar. Then throw a little curve ball here and there and respond faster or take even longer than normal to respond to keep your messages unpredictable. That will keep her always anticipating your response, she will be looking at her phone wondering when you will text back. Doing this will keep the interaction level similar and no one will look weird responding within minutes while the other takes their sweet time making the other wait. If she happens to be a very consistent texter, mirror your response times close to hers as well but never forget to have her anticipate your message every so often. The key here is you cannot make yourself seem too available or too unavailable. Responding immediately every time can turn her off just as much as taking hours to respond every time can too.

Self-Esteem

As mentioned before, the energy you give off always needs to be of high confidence online and in-person. By that I mean you literally need to feel confident, not act like it. Faking it until you make it can only get you so far because self-esteem is more than just words behind a phone, it is the overall vibe that matters. Women can read in between the lines and have that sixth sense; they can feel if you are a grounded man or a man who has not found his base yet. Never feel you are beneath a woman and never doubt your self-worth feeling the need to seek her validation, you are in control of your emotions, not her. But most of all, never lower your standards for anyone, and I mean anyone. Women will cut a man off for the smallest reasons and that is because they know they have a ton of options; you need to be the exact same way. Set your standards high and never feel the need to settle for anything less than you deserve. Embedding that sense of abundance will only favor you in the long run, I can assure you that.

If you do not like a woman who responds every six hours, do not put up with it and stop communication. If she acts smart with you, do not be scared to act smart back. If you hate one-word answers or vague responses and she does it often, leave her on read or like the message and do not respond. You do not know how many times I have done that to a woman of interest and funny thing is, most have openly told me it makes them feel some type of way. Only because women ignore and cut men off all the time, and a man having the balls to do it back will make you stick out like a sore thumb to her. Women cannot stand it, especially if she has interest in you and is trying to play games seeking your validation. To her, that shows you are rejecting her and will make her question things creating a need of validation from you now. That is when you will see her double text or give you a call days later looking to communicate again. Even though no one likes being ignored or left on read, it needs to be done to let her know you do not play games. Except many men do not have the balls do that, they will settle for how the woman is believing they cannot do better or try to change who they are just to satisfy her. Women know how persistent and needy men can be, so they become comfortable and sit back with a smile positive you will keep coming back around which is exactly why doing it to them hurts their ego so much. A lot of men will text back repeatedly waiting for a response giving them the validation they seek. So, from this moment on, you must be a one and done type of texter and that is it. As I mentioned before, too much attention will demonstrate you are a fan, not a potential dating interest. That is a big turn off to most women, and most men scratch their heads wondering "what did I do? I'm supposed to pursue her right?" Yes, to an extent you do need to pursue a woman whether it be online or in-person but showing desperation is where you need to stop and think. Many men see chasing as going for what you want but there is a fine line between being persistent for the time being and looking like a stalker in the long run. Chasing non-stop demonstrates you are needy, and you will always be there when she has no other options, putting you at the back of the line as a last case resort. Forcing any sort of conversation ends bad either way so if it does not flow organically, it is not worth your effort.

     I am confident that if you stand your ground when the time is appropriate, she will respect your standards and you will see her start changing her ways of communicating with you. Women know what they are doing, they know most men are desperate and will put up with anything just to get her into bed. Little do they know that is the best way to lose a woman's respect and attraction to begin with. A real woman wants a man with high value, not a weak-minded man that allows himself to be a puppet unless she is truly dominant as I mentioned before. Show her you are there to get to know her, but also show her you are not afraid to walk away if she does not meet your requirements too. But most of all, never chase her for a conversation no matter what. If she does not respond to you, *do not* text her again and leave it like it is. If she has high enough interest in you, she will reach out, believe me. Therefore, you need to be a man of abundance and never be afraid to give off the energy that you have options and standards. Giving off a solid confident vibe early in the texting stage is a great way to increase attraction and her attention. Nothing turns a woman on more than a man who knows what he has to offer and refuses to settle for less, it shows *you* are the catch and will make you her first choice.

Conversational Connection Points (CCP)

Conversational Connection Points are bits of information someone gives you during an interaction that allows to relate and respond to it to further extend the conversation. This is the key to successfully building repour with a woman quickly and effectively. You do this by asking a question, taking a piece of information from their response, and relating to it in order form trust and a deeper connection. A CCP is what makes a conversation flow, without it the entire interaction will seem very robotic, and you will end up getting nowhere with it. Correctly using CCP's will bring any common interests and beliefs you may share to the forefront building repour quickly. However, do not be afraid to disagree with something she tells you. That not only shows you have your own opinions, but it will make the conversation more interesting on both ends. Being able to voice your opinion and stand by it is a trait they find incredibly attractive in men. If you agree with everything, she will see you as insincere thinking you are telling her everything she wants to hear, never be afraid to spice the conversation up if it remains cordial. You must pay attention to the details in what she says, that is the key to having exceptional conversational skills with women, they like to know you listen. Once you master the art of identifying CCP's and executing them accordingly, you will find it extremely easy to build a connection with a woman of potential interest. If you are already good at communicating feel free to skip this part, but if you feel unsure, keep reading.

CCP Example:

This is a real conversation I had with a woman. After initiating the conversation with an indirect approach, I noticed she engaged well in the conversation, so I decided to change the subject and further the interaction.

Me: "I see you post a lot of pictures in Colombia, are you from there?"

Her: "Yes! My family is from Cali, Colombia. I was born and raised there I miss it...but I do visit often!"

Me: "I was in Colombia a few months ago actually! I loved it, the culture and food in Colombia was on point too. I can see where the beauty comes from then, the women in Colombia are flawless haha"

Her: "That's awesome... I miss my country so much I'm glad you liked it. As for the women, thank you! I guess it's in our genetics ;) What about you handsome, where are you from?"

Me: "You're welcome love, as for me I was raised in Upstate New York in the countryside, and now currently in Orlando, Florida. As for my ethnicity, I'm Puerto Rican."

Her: "Now I can see where you get your looks from as well, I love Puerto Rican men haha. I'm actually planning a trip there with my girls this summer, what do you recommend seeing?"

End Conversation

As you can see, connecting CCP's is simple. I asked her a question, found a piece of information in her response that allowed me to make a connection, and then threw in some light flirtation to top it off (which is optional). In this example, I really did go to Colombia, so it was the perfect opportunity to connect with her especially when she emphasized how much she missed it. At the end of it all she started engaging a lot more when she saw there was common interests to speak on, before it was mainly small talk. As you can also see, every response I had did not end with a question either, doing that will allow her to freely respond and put effort in herself. Asking too many questions will not give her the opportunity to openly speak, so always give some space allowing her to naturally respond and give you connection points to leverage without dragging it out of her. Finding that initial connection point is the crucial spark you need to get a woman truly invested in the conversation. No matter what a woman says during an interaction, you can always find a CCP to leverage during a conversation or ask the right questions to get them out of her. Remember, CCP's are extremely important to use whether it is online or in person on an actual date. They will act as the basic building blocks while you are getting to know someone until the conversation flows organically. You will not only be great at forming conversations with substance, but you will learn how to ask penetrating questions that will get her fully engaged. The goal is to get her to the point where she is talking mostly about herself, that is when you know you have her emotionally invested.

Adding value to a conversation is the best way to build repour with a woman. The faster you can make her comfortable talking to you, the faster she will go out on a date. It also gives you the upper hand to call her out if she does not give you the same value back. If you are speaking to a woman and you see she is being bland or not very responsive, I would give it no more than three attempts to spark any real interaction. After that, you are wasting your time because it means she is simply not interested in talking or she is just looking for attention, and no man with value accepts that. Be bold, if she sucks at conversations and expects you to ask all the questions, do not be afraid to call a woman out on her lack of conversational skills. If she does not like your opinion then too bad, because I bet you anything, you will be one of the few that has the confidence to tell her like it is. The goal is to address it without disrespecting her and she will never have a good enough reason to use that against you. So do not worry if she gets upset, she will come back around if she likes you. It may not happen the next day, but soon enough she will end up messaging you or give indirect signals to shoot your shot again such as liking random posts or commenting on your stories. If she does not, then it is totally fine because you are actively talking to other women and do not have time to think about it. Even if you are not talking to multiple women, being that fearless and indifferent will make your self-assurance grow, proving you have high value.

Voice Messages

Voice messages can be a good way to add variety to a conversation. Knowing the sound of your voice can create a quicker connection since the interaction becomes a lot more personalized that way. Send her voice messages *sparingly* to make the conversation a little more personable and interesting, it works every time. It is a good opportunity to show her your personality ahead of time so when you meet, she already knows what to expect which will cut out that awkward stage at the beginning of a date immediately. I am not saying to send her a five-minute-long voice message because no one will listen to that, that is a little too much. Just use the voice messages when it fits the scenario in the conversation, especially if you are joking around or speaking about a more serious topic. Sometimes it is easier to express yourself with a quick voice message to get your point across.

Sexual Flirtation

Sexual flirtation is something that must happen to further the relationship with any woman especially if you want something more intimate with her. If not, you will be building a very cozy home in the friendzone, trust me. Women are not like men, they cannot get an erection like us and immediately be ready to go, sometimes it takes more preparation for that sexual tension to build up. Women love the erotic process, which usually starts with small, sexual thoughts until it escalates to the point where that sexual tension is ready to be released. Those initial thoughts usually start when she notices certain characteristics about a man she believes are attractive or by doing specific actions she thinks are sexy. Some examples of that can be the way you naturally take initiative, your body, the way you touch her leg during conversation, or even because you do a masculine act like fix a flat tire. Masculine traits like that will naturally increase a woman's attraction and start planting sexual thoughts in her head. Women get turned on by the series of events that lead up to sex, so playing along with that narrative will get her to the point where she jumps your bones the moment you seduce her.

     Don't worry, planting those sexual seeds can be accomplished using the right language during messaging as well. Since you will be approaching her via Instagram, any physical flirting will not be able to happen at first. So, the best way to approach sexual flirting while messaging is by using direct or indirect sexual statements. Just keep in mind flirting online can be tricky, being sexually flirtatious too soon before she is comfortable will make her think you are perverted, and some women get into it sooner. Read her boundaries before making that move, as I mentioned before, it is usually a gradual process until she is fully comfortable with direct sexual flirtation. Coming on too strong before you have even met or spoken for a decent amount of time will make you seem desperate for sex to some women, take the level of flirtation gradually. The only way coming on strong at first will work is if she has very high interest in you from the start and shows it, if not, it is best to work your way up. Test the waters, you can do so by giving complements that make her feel good about herself inside and out seeing the type of response she gives. Without any sexual tension or any type of flirtation for that matter, your conversations will never pass that friendship level. You must show her you are interested and that she can trust you, there are many people with bad intentions out there or people faking to be someone else. Women are all different when it comes to flirting, some will escalate quickly to sexual flirting, and some take more time to feel comfortable with it. When you see a great chance to sexually flirt, do not hesitate to do so when you feel the moment is right and the confidence is there. When the right time comes, they are usually waiting for you to cross that line since most of them fear to be judged negatively by you or other people, it is what they call an *anti-slut defense*. If you are not familiar with what an anti-slut defense is, it is when a woman negates any sexual comment or advancement in fear of being seen as easy or a slut. Women think about sex too, only thing is, they have their own way on how they deal with it.

      There are endless amounts of compliments to tell her whether it is directly sexual or not to get her mind going, I will share some momentarily. My only advice is when you are not flirting sexually, make sure it is about her looks, personality, or anything she is passionate about and you are golden. If you state them with confidence and sex appeal, you will not come off as corny or insecure which is the most important part with flirting in general. To demonstrate, I will show an example of an actual conversation I had on how to test the waters with a woman and get her mind thinking. It is a key aspect of any flirtation between two people. In this example, I had already approached her via Instagram and at this point we were text messaging and having consistent conversations. I was planning a night out to meet up for drinks, so I took the opportunity to see where I could take the interaction. I planted the seed, and saw her sexual thoughts grow.

Sexual Flirtation Example:

Me: "Ready for tonight? I have a spot already picked out; it's a chill place with an outside balcony, you're going to love it."

Her: "Yes I am! I'm wearing a simple, yet dressy outfit so it seems like it's appropriate for the place. I really hope it's not going to be super-hot tonight if we sit outside :("

Me: "Yea I know me too; I don't think it's going to be too hot though. If not, I might have to do a corny strip show and hangout butt naked to keep cool haha"

Her: "You wouldn't do that lol"

Me: "Wanna make a bet?"

Her: "What are we betting on?! Lol jk. If you did, I'd have to start charging all the girls for pictures with the attention you'd be getting lmao"

Me: "That might be a good side hustle though...it might make you a few extra thousand a night lol"

Her: "Right? I'll make money and enjoy the view as well. If the money is that good, we might need to move the business to my place to attract more paying customers lol"

Me: "I'm with it, just make sure you don't let anyone take advantage of me while I'm all naked in your house..."

Her: "They wouldn't be allowed to put their hands on you! If one girl does then they're all getting kicked out, and then guess what? I'll have that view all to myself."

Me: "If that's the case then you're getting naked too, it has to be even so we both can enjoy the view ;)"

Her: "You and I naked sounds like trouble..."

Me: "Well, let's just say it's the only trouble you won't regret getting into ;)"

Her: "Lol oh really?!?! Then let's see what trouble we get into tonight, see you soon handsome."

End Conversation

As you can see, I tested the waters to see how she would react. After she gave a positive response to my indirect sexual statement, I decided to roll with it further. A simple word such as "naked" will get her mind thinking, I took her comment about the weather being hot as the perfect opportunity. Sometimes it only takes one word to escalate the sexual tension quickly, it is all about planting the seed and taking the necessary steps to make it grow. Single words can be good at the beginning to feel her boundaries since you can use them indirectly like I did in the example. Later, you can move on to direct questions and statements once you have established a solid continuous conversation.

Whether it is intentional or not, women will give you little windows of opportunity for you to sexually flirt if you do it correctly and pay attention. Even if she had not given in and started flirting sexually, an indirect line or word as such will not do any harm regardless. When it is time to be bold, using sexual questions and statements work best when they fit the conversational scenario, but never push your boundaries if you see she is not giving you positive feedback. Using direct lines will show her you are not afraid to be forward, a lot of men fear being rejected so they never bother to try coming off as shy. Being forward turns a woman on, it shows her you speak your mind without hesitation. To help you out, below are some lines you can use to get her thinking sexually, use them wisely and use them as inspiration for new ones. Women love excitement and unpredictability, so lay the heat on her when the time is right and the repour is there. I guarantee you will see her engagement blow through the roof during a conversation. As I mentioned before, they love the erotic process, so once you get her to this point the chances of getting her out is very high because she will be very intrigued.

Here are lines you can use:

- What do you normally wear to bed?
- Do you prefer sleeping naked or wearing a t-shirt to bed?
- How important is sex in a relationship to you?
- I was asked this today by a friend; how many days a week should a couple have sex? I said (place response here) What do you think?
- What do you like to wear that makes you feel sexy?
- What's your favorite part of a man's body?
- Do you enjoy full body massages?

- What turns you on about a guy that isn't common?
- What's something non-sexual that turns you on?
- Are you an aggressive or passionate kisser?
- Do you like to cuddle?
- What's your ultimate sexual fantasy?
- Could you cuddle naked without wanting anything more?
- What are your sensitive spots?
- Pool sex or jacuzzi sex? What would turn you on more?
- Do you watch porn? What's your go-to category?
- What's something crazy you've done no one knows about?
- A woman who's adventurous is sexy to me, how adventurous are you?
- What's better, food or orgasms?

Use these at the right moment, and it will make the conversation much more interesting for the both of you. Remember, there are endless phrases you can use, these are just a few to piggyback from.

Extra Advice:

- ✓ If the chemistry is there, do not take exaggeratedly long to start flirting sexually. Lagging on too long will either turn her off or make her think you see her as a friend and move on.
- ✓ Do not be too graphic with your lines at first, sometimes women can get uncomfortable quickly especially if she does not know you too well and feels you are sexualizing her. If you have already had sex or are dating, anything is fair game. Or, if the sexual

chemistry is strong and clear between you guys, being ballsy will not hurt you at that point either.
- ✓ If you do not feel comfortable being direct at first, start small and as you see her giving positive feedback, ask her more direct questions moving forward. As I said before, unless obvious sexual chemistry is present from the start, working your way up is the safer route unless you do not care what the outcome is.
- ✓ If you choose to be bold and ask her direct sexual questions from the start, it will either work in your favor or she will get creeped out. Keep caution and try to read her before making that kind of move and be aware of the potential consequences. Paying attention to her words and flirtation levels are the best indicators.
- ✓ Words and phrases such as naked, hot, wet, hard, orgasm, bad ass, sexy, mouth, lips, are words you can throw in casually in texting that can indirectly set her off. Use these in normal texts by blending them in subliminally and that will be a great start.

Qualification Questions and Statements

Qualification questions and statements are the male version of a womans shit tests, it is our way of pre-screening her to see if she meets our standards. Women will test you in forms of questions or actions to see how you measure as a man and is something that will happen regardless, whether she is dominant for submissive. Some will purposely shit test you and some subconsciously shit test you. They will ask specific questions or do certain actions to measure your character and security as a man all depending on how you respond. For example, they may ask specific questions on relationships and judge you based on your response. Such as how many women you have slept with or your opinion on how a man should act within a relationship. Or they may do actions such as turning their face when you go in for a kiss even though she has shown signs of high interest just to test your reaction. If you get angry or defensive, they see you as insecure, but if you play it cool and calm, they see you as confident. Shit tests come in various forms and paying close attention to her questions and actions will be the best way to catch onto them quickly. Except overall, they do it to evaluate your worthiness and social status to her, because as I mentioned previously in this book, they are the choosers. That is exactly why men should do the same thing and test women on their worthiness to us as well. Qualifying is the best way to show her you are a man of high value and standards. Most men are scared to qualify a woman due to the potential backlash, but this is the best way to show you have confidence and get her to prove herself to you.

There are two main goals for qualifying a woman:

1) Test her character and confidence
2) Gain her respect

Unfortunately, qualifying will only work when you see a sign of interest on her end. If you try to qualify without signs of interest, she will most likely get offended or pull the "toxic masculinity "card on you. But if she does show signs of interest and you can qualify her correctly, it will increase attraction because it shows her you are bold, which is an alpha characteristic. The byproduct of qualifying a woman correctly will undoubtedly increase her attraction level towards you but most of all, it will make her respect you. Without respect, no woman will take you seriously in the long run. A lot of men believe they are not being a gentleman by having any sort of backbone towards a woman, but that is the furthest thing from the truth. And that ties into what I mentioned earlier in this book, we are raised in a society that teaches us to be the type of men women are not attracted to. If you cannot challenge her or at least defend yourself when she shit tests you, she will never respect you leading to her losing attraction in the future. The men that get loads of women drooling over them, chasing them, or even fighting over them, are the ones who have an abundance mindset and are respected by the opposite sex. They will qualify and set a woman in her place immediately if needed, and they will never be afraid to leave and move on to another if she does not meet his standards. Which is why you will never see a man who has the "happy wife, happy life" mentality have any form of concrete respect from a woman. They were shit tested from the start and miserably failed, leaving them with zero power and respect from their significant other. That is why qualifying a woman is so important from the beginning! Not only does it build attraction, but it sets the tone letting her know you will never allow her walk all over you and doing that keeps a woman enticed and on her toes.

Extra Advice:

- ✓ Whenever you qualify a woman, it is important to sometimes solidify the situation by ending it with a light compliment or a positive qualifying statement. The point is not to make her feel beneath you or not good enough, keep that in mind. I will show you an example of that soon.
- ✓ Women who purposefully shit-test men will know you are trying to qualify her, so be prepared because she will qualify you right back. You must know how to adapt and work your way around it, and never give in by feeling the need to qualify yourself to keep her

at ease, she will lose respect for you immediately. Do not push it to the point where you are both pissed off but stand your ground and think before you speak, acting indifferent is key. Being cool, calm, and collected is always the way to go.

✓ If you qualify during messaging, again, be aware of how easily things can be misconstrued and taken a different way so be careful and try not to sound too offensive or overbearing. If you use these in person, make sure you do not act aggressive. Acting aggressive will make you look crazy and make her feel uncomfortable, say them in a slightly playful way but keep your masculine energy strong so she knows you still mean business while asking.

Qualification Example #1:

This is a girl I added on social media and turns out we go to the same gym. We would engage on each other's stories exchanging flirtatious compliments often, so it was apparent the interest was mutual. I wanted to set up a workout date but only thing is, she would not say much during our conversations wanting me to put in all the effort and ask all the questions. Personally, a woman who expects the man to chase her for conversation is a huge pet peeve. So, here is how I worked my way around that to get her to engage more by calling her out on her lack of conversational skills making her prove herself to me. This line can be used for a situation like this where she is vague with her responses or throws you the annoying "lol" or a one-word answer often. It is not the traditional way of asking a qualifying question, but it serves the same purpose by gaining her respect and making her prove herself to you.

Me: "I see you hit the gym a lot, It's a big passion?"

Her: "Yea!"

Me: "Haha cool, I'm all about the gym as well. A woman who's fit & healthy is always a plus, I love that."

Her: "Haha, thanks."

Me: "You're welcome. So, I'm going to the gym tomorrow in the evening. That's around the time you go right? Let's get a workout in, I can use a good partner for leg day."

Her: "ok"

Me: "Hmm, you don't say much, do you? I never thought an attractive woman like yourself would have such little to say during a conversation, I didn't expect that from you."

Her: "lol...what do you mean? That's not fair to say..."

Her: "I talk a lot actually...like a lot."

Her: "Maybe not the best texter though...I'm sorry I came off like that I actually can talk your ears off lol"

Her: "Lets workout tomorrow then? What time works for you??"

Me: "No worries, but 7pm works for me, try not to outlift me I see the weight you squat lol see you tomorrow."

End Conversation

See how that conversation flipped the moment I gave her a qualification statement that made her feel the need to explain herself to me? I gave her three chances to start engaging but she kept replying with the same vague responses as she did before with our conversations, so I had enough and called her out on it. She went from responding to how she wanted, to justifying why she could not hold a decent conversation. When you use this line, you need to say it with disappointment since you are letting her know she is walking on thin ice and starting to lose your interest. A lot of women will be interested in you but will want you to chase her for her attention, it all has to do with their naturally built abundance mindset with men. Hit her with that line or anything similar and it will make her not only qualify herself, but it will let her know you are not afraid to call her out. This tactic works a lot, so never be scared to lay it on her. After, she will put forth more effort while talking to you respecting your thoughts. But if she does not change, drop her because she is not worth your time at that point. Conversations should be equal, not a one-sided interaction.

Qualification Example #2:

In this example, I will show you how to ask a qualification question. These are used mostly when you are casually talking to her and see a window of opportunity to qualify her on a certain standard you have. Avoid being too serious while qualifying this way, and never ask her question after question as if you are interrogating her. Be cool and collected while you qualify her just like any normal conversation and you will be golden. In this situation I was talking to a girl and the subject of dating came up, so I asked her a qualifying question about my dating beliefs to test what her response would be. We already had repour built up, so this sort of qualifying is best when you see she is willing to speak on personal matters.

Me: "So how long have you been single?"

Her: "It's been less than a year since I broke up with my ex. How about you?"

Me: "Ok not too long I see. For me I would say the same, a little less than a year. What happened? Did he drive you crazy? Lol give me the inside scoop."

Her: "He was just too insecure; I couldn't have one guy look at me or take too long to reply before he would start an argument. I basically got fed up with it lmao.

Her: "How about you, why did you and your ex call it quits? Not going to lie, you look like the heart breaker type haha"

Me: "Damn that's how you see me? Haha I'm playing around, but basically I broke up with her because she would get annoyed whenever I wanted to take a night and spend time with family..."

Me: *"I'm a very family-oriented person and I couldn't be with someone who is bothered by me spending time with them. How about you, what is your take on family?*

Her: "Oh no I totally understand, I'm a family person too! I would never be mad if you were to spend time with your family if I were her, that's unfair and selfish. I love that you're like that though, that's very attractive."

Me: "Ok good! I'm happy we're on the same page then, I think we'll get along just fine."

End Conversation

That is one of many ways you can qualify a woman with a question. Can you see how smooth it came out casually during conversation? That is the best way to qualify a woman without her noticing at all during an interaction. Remember, a lot of women are in tune with their shit testing and if you make it obvious, she is going to figure it out fast. Here, I took the opportunity to see what her view on family was, so I let her know I do not date women who are bothered by me spending time with family. As you can see, she fell into my qualifier and elaborated on how she would never do that if that were her and gave me a compliment to top it all off. As a reward for her passing my qualifier, I validated her response by letting her know I was happy she agreed with me. Not giving some sort of validation or assurance at the end will only give off the vibe that you think you are better than her, which is not the goal here. The goal is to make her open up to you and prove she meets your dating standards without her even realizing it. Qualifying questions and statements are a man's secret weapon, but they should only be used when the appropriate time comes, and you see a window of opportunity. Qualifying her too much will make you look narcissistic, and that will raise a red flag to her immediately. You do not always have to ask a direct question when qualifying, it can be in the form of a statement by casually saying your qualifier seeing if she bites the bait and responds to it. Be illusive as possible with it, and you will see the positive results that follow.

Here are some good qualification examples:

- You're really attractive, but are you humble? That's hard to find.
- An ambitious woman is sexy, what are your future goals?
- My weakness for food is my biggest downfall, do you cook?
- I'm the adventurous type, how adventurous are you?
- I prefer a woman who thinks loyalty is key in any relationship, what's your opinion?

- You seem like a handful; how will I be sure you won't drive me crazy in the long run? (Be humorous with this one)
- I like you, but do you work out? I love a woman who is in tune with her health.
- You don't say much, do you? I never thought an attractive woman like you would have such little to say.
- Do you (Insert pet peeve)? That's one of my deal breakers with women.
- I'm a family man, what is your view on family?
- What's your ideal relationship? I'm curious if we're on the same page
- What are the top three qualities about yourself?
- What's something you're proud of that you never really tell people?
- I love an independent woman; would you consider yourself independent?
- You seem like the partying type, what else do you do for fun besides that?
- I see you're not much of a conversationalist, are you like that in person as well?
- You seem like a firecracker which is attractive, but are you easy going too? I love easy going girls also

Extra Advice:

- ✓ Use these when they fit into the conversation, whether you set the conversation up to ask them or it comes up naturally.
- ✓ Some are light qualifiers, and some are stern, use the stern ones when you see she gives attitude, tests you, or does something that turns you off.

- ✓ These are general ones you can use; you can reword them any way you want. These are examples I have used myself but there are countless ways to use qualification questions and statements.
- ✓ If she hits you back with her own qualification question, do not elaborate in full detail. Give her a generalized, concrete response, do not end up being the one qualifying yourself instead in elaborate detail. Being open is fine but leave her crumbs and not the whole cookie so to speak, women are attracted to mystery.

Humor

We all know women like humor, but how much humor is enough? Everyone knows that guy in grade-school who was the class clown but never had a girlfriend or any woman wanting him. If you are always acting like a clown, she will take you as the friend who makes her laugh and throw you in the friendzone. A woman wants a man who is funny and sexy, most men who only play the clown card are taken as a best friend because they do not know how to balance the two. I am not saying to be boring, because you must be able to make a woman laugh to get her fully comfortable with you. Except there must be a balance between the two, and that is the key to keeping your humor and sex appeal equally alive. Acting like a fool every time you are around her will not show her you are a masculine man, it will show her you are a comedian for her entertainment. Being a man who is humorous with strong sex appeal will have women drooling over you non-stop. It shows her you can joke around and be playful, but also take care of business romantically. Whether you are talking to a girl online or in-person, never forget to have that healthy balance between the two. Take notes and watch movies where the man is humorous but still has strong sex appeal. Movies with actors such as Mathew McConaughey, Brad Pitt, and Leonardo DiCaprio are great examples on how to be make a woman laugh yet have strong sex appeal to your game at the same time.

I have a friend who always plays the clown card, he tries to be the comedian doing the most to be the center of attention. He is the type that makes constant jokes, funny faces, and gets drunk and starts doing outrageous things. To be honest he is hilarious, and he knows how to lift the mood in any group, so it's always fun to be around him especially on those crazy nights out. He would not act like the clown all the time, but he would always become one if girls were present at that moment. His reasoning for being the clown was because he assumed it was making up for the fact that he was not gifted with model looks and six-pack abs. He thought playing the clown card was his only way to attract women. Well, he was completely wrong, and that is why he saw himself year after year without a girlfriend or long-lasting love interest. I kept telling him why and how to fix it, but he would never take my advice into consideration and continued with the same cycle repeatedly.

I will give him credit, he managed to land numerous women from dating apps, but most of them would leave him in the friendzone after the first few dates or play with his feelings giving him no respect. His belief in the concept "girls fall for funny guys" was taken too literal, he failed to realize there needed to be a balance between humor and sex appeal. I have seen funny guys more hideous than Freddy Kruger land women who look like models. Why? Because at the end of the day they know a woman wants a man, not just a clown for her entertainment. They know how to balance humor with game to form that genuine attraction with a woman. Be humorous and make her laugh, but do not overdo it like a clown, and never forget to maintain your sex appeal so you can keep that romantic attraction alive. Never depend on humor to get her to like you because eventually that humor will keep going while the attraction she has will not.

Chapter 8: Closing on the Date

You have all the tools you need to find women, approach them, and have successful conversations with them. Now it is time to ask a girl out, exchange numbers, and take her out on a date. This is the moment men fear the most whether it is in person or online, but it is the moment you need to be fearless with to date the women you really want. You might feel unconfident asking a girl out due to the possible rejection factor of it all but being scared is only going to hurt you in the long run. A lot of women you approach online will accept your advances, and yet again many will not, it is all part of dating. It has happened to me, and it has happened to many other men, it's life. You can look like a model and still get rejected, so if you fear rejection remember than no one, and I mean no one, is fully protected from it. It happens to everyone in some shape or form.

You also must keep in mind that women are normally more selective than men by nature, and that is a fact. It might not seem that way since you have probably seen the same woman dating a different guy every other week, but as I mentioned earlier, women get a lot more attention from men on average than we do from them. Why? Because men are scientifically proven to be more sexual than women due to the amount of testosterone in our bodies compared to theirs. Ever heard of the saying that men tend to think with the head below their waist and not with the one above their shoulders? That is because testosterone is the main hormone that directly correlates to sexual desire. We have more testosterone in our bodies than they do which is exactly why men are known as the seed spreaders, the chasers, and the pursuers. If you were to post a shirtless picture half naked in a towel and get five new messages in your inbox, a woman who posts a picture of her ass in lingerie will have three times as many messages from men in hers. So, if a woman tries to tell you they are more sexual than men, they are lying. Unless she injects testosterone, can grow a mustache and choke slam you like she is in the WWE, I would believe science before a woman who tells you otherwise. Anyways, my point here is women are more selective naturally, and since many have loads of men waiting in line to take them out, she will give priority to the man who meets her preferred type first. So never feel bad if you get rejected after asking a girl out, we all have our preferences and types, that is what makes us human in the end. You cannot win every time, and that is why it is a numbers game when it is all said and done in the world of dating.

Rejection

I wanted to make a section to address rejection, because it is one of the most important factors on why men avoid making a move. If a woman rejects you, just learn from it, you can learn a lot from every interaction with a woman whether it is a failure or success. I know for many of you, rejection goes a lot deeper than that, maybe you had a traumatic experience or saw a friend get rejected making you imagine how it would feel. Except the simple thought of seeing rejection as a learning curve more than a disaster will help you grow a healthier viewpoint towards it. As I mentioned, no one is safe from rejection, so why would you keep hiding or running away from it?

We all have horrible rejection stories, so I will share my most embarrassing one with you. The worst rejection I have ever faced was the time I got denied at a local spot one night out with my friend. My friend and I had been bar hopping when he saw a girl he thought was cute while walking by this bar, so we turned around and went in to check it out. The girl was standing at the bar with her friend, so he suggested approaching them since they were the only women of interest within the vicinity after briefly scoping out the room. I personally was not feeling it, only because these two women were at the bar comfortably posted up. If you see a girl or group of girls posted up at the bar for no reason, there is a good chance they are waiting for men to come and offer them free drinks. Those are the type of women you want to avoid unless you are ready to dish out money for nothing in return. I can spot women like that from a mile away, they are the ones alone at the bar looking pretty the entire night socializing with no one except for the guys asking them if they want a drink. But, since my friend was adamant about speaking to this girl, I gave in, and we began walking towards them. At that point I took a good look at the friend, and she was absolutely beautiful, so I warmed up to the idea and saw it as a good opportunity. Except as we approached and I said hello to her friend, she barely looked me in the eyes. She was very bland and short with her responses and quite frankly, came off very rude. You can tell the interest level of any woman within seconds after approaching her, and it was obvious her interest was low. Although the interaction was not going well, I kept my confidence and was sure I can flip her uninterest since she was an attractive woman, I had nothing to lose and saw it as a challenge. But then it all took a turn for the worse, and after speaking for around a minute or so, she yelled, "this conversation is really fucking annoying me, go away" and danced as she turned back around towards the bar. It was the hardest, most unexpected public rejection I have gone through. She never even let me finish speaking; she ended the conversation mid-sentence while I stood there with the words in my mouth.

Not only did half the people at the bar hear her, but so did my friend as he held back his laughter. She basically made me look and feel like an idiot and it was embarrassing to say the least.

Worst part of all, as I look to the side after being torn to shreds by her rejection, I locked eyes with another girl I coincidentally had been speaking to online just a few days prior. I never noticed she was there, and ironically, we had planned to meet up for drinks the following weekend. As you could have guessed, she saw the whole thing and let's just say that date her and I planned never happened. Turned out they both knew each other and since she saw me get verbally manhandled by her friend, it turned her off and I basically got rejected by two girls at the same time. Yes, I was sour about it but to be honest it was just bad timing and bad luck all the way around. Thankfully, I bounced back later at a different spot and ended the night on a good note leaving the place with another woman I met. But what did I learn from that night? To start, I should have taken her signals of disinterest as a sign to exit the interaction sooner even though I have been able to flip a woman's disinterest before in the past. But the biggest lesson learned was the fact that not every woman will like you and not every woman you approach will end in success. I used to be prideful at times and think, how can you reject me? Who do you think you are? And that is something I had to come to terms with so I could get over that hurdle of rejection. Some men are prideful with rejection and some men are genuinely hurt by rejection; whichever side you fall on needs to be accepted for what it is.

There will be times where the girl you really want does not want you back, whether she gave you a shot and moved on or never gave you a chance at all. There will also be girls that really like you but unfortunately you do not like them back either. The sooner you accept that reality, the sooner you will get over the fear of rejection. It may take a few times to be fully numb to it, but I promise you, not caring about rejection will only boost your confidence even more. If someone rejects you, always remember what you bring to the table, and never let anyone make you feel like you aren't good enough. The energy of not giving a shit is what makes a confident man glow and will make you attract more women hands down no matter if they reject you or not. At that point there is nothing anyone can do that will get to you; you will feel mighty and a lot more opportunities will arise since women will feel that energy. If I went through that embarrassing rejection in person and bounced back you can bounce back from anything, especially if it is on Instagram.

Whether you are rejected or not by a woman, that same woman has been rejected by men who she liked but did not like her in return. If any woman says otherwise, she is lying, because everyone has been rejected at some point in their life. I will let you in on a secret; *women fear rejection just as much or more than men do.* Which is why most women cringe at the thought of approaching a man they believe is attractive, they fear getting shot down and their ego hurt just as much. Rejection goes both ways; I have gone on dates with girls I met online and never heard from them again and I have done the same with other women as well. It will happen whether you like it or not, especially if you begin dating often. People are different in their own ways, you cannot expect to fully satisfy every single woman you meet, it does not work like that. You can choose to let it bring you down or make you not care even more, so never feel bewildered if you fear rejection. Going through dating hiccups will help you learn from rejection better, giving you time to process and desensitize yourself from it. Be a man of abundance and take pride in what you have to offer! If you want to date beautiful women consistently, you must put yourself on your own pedestal.

The Close

After speaking for a while, you will have a certain timeframe to ask for her number while she is fully invested in the conversation. Stalling too long will make her lose interest and if she does, the chances of a second chance are slim. Never keep her waiting on you to make a move if the signs are there, or she will not hesitate to pass her number to the guy taking full initiative, remember that. Some anticipation is good, but after days or weeks of her waiting, she will put you in the friend zone or stop responding. The only thing you can do is feel out the energy of the conversation and pinpoint the right time to ask for her number. It is crucial to read her overall vibe or any indirect signals she throws your way to make the move. You might wonder how you can "feel" that out, but as you speak to more women consistently, you will be able to pick apart the ones who have solid interest and the ones who do not. Women with solid interest normally flirt back and have interactive conversations with you, while those who do not have solid interest will ignore you, make excuses when you ask them out, and rarely flirt back. They will also take extremely long to answer every time never letting the conversation pass the small talk stage. Those are more obvious signals to pay attention to and consider.

As for indirect signals, a lot of women will say they are in the mood for a drink or tell you they have been dying to do a certain activity like movies or dinner. Since most women expect to be pursued, they always wait for your move or say certain things indirectly to motivate you to ask her out. Except be careful with those signals, they can be insincere if it comes from the wrong type of person. Always make sure her interest is real; some women go on dates for the free food and drinks only to disappear or keep you at arms-length contacting you only when she wants something else. Never allow a woman to take advantage of you, there are many out there who only look for what you can offer them on a date. And if a woman invites *you* out, make sure the bill is split or she takes care of it. There are women who will ask you out to that fancy dinner or big concert and have the audacity to try and make you pay for it. You are NEVER obligated to pay if a woman asks you out, so never be scared to ask for separate bills because many women try to take you for an idiot on purpose. They will use the "be a gentleman" excuse after they have intentionally done the same exact thing to countless others. Therefore, due to the variables, it is up to you to feel her energy and correctly read her signals for you to step up or avoid her, there is nothing else to it. As I mentioned before, always go with your hunch no matter what, you will feel when a woman's interests are sincere or not so trust your instincts. But most of all, when you find a good date opportunity and ask her out, speak with confidence and take control of the interaction. You need to insinuate she will say yes to your date proposal right then and there. If that is slightly confusing let me show you an example on how to do it, and how not to do it.

Wrong way to ask: *"So, I was wondering...may I have your number? Maybe we can hang out this weekend or maybe sometime soon possibly? Only if you want to."*

Notice how weak that sounds? If you ask a woman out like this, you might as well get comfortable in the friendzone because you are never getting out. You are not only looking weak, but you are showing her you can't even ask her out with confidence. Using too many doubt words and insecure questions is the wrong way to ask a woman out, especially if she has other men doing it correctly. She will see you as a low value male and will immediately be turned off by the thought of getting to know you on a romantic level. The odds of a second chance will be non-existent unless she tries to take advantage and use you for the free food and drinks.

Right way to ask: *"You seem pretty down to earth; I would love to meet you. Let's exchange numbers and I'll plan a nice date for us; we can go out this upcoming weekend."*

See how affirmative that is? I started off by validating her, letting her know she is worth my time and fits my standards. After that, I asked for her number and confidently told her I was taking her out that upcoming weekend. The point is not to ask a woman out with a question, but with a firm suggestion. It shows her you are direct and not scared to go for what you want. Even if she ends up telling you she cannot make it that weekend, it shows you are assertive. A woman who is interested will let you know when she is free, even if the day you picked does not work out for her at first. Do not feel bewildered if she does not fully bite the bait right away, the fact that you pursued her with confidence is all you need to seal the date. They love a man who can act like one, not a man who is not straight forward and cannot take the lead. Do this, and she will already have a level of respect for you before you even meet, and that is an incredible way to start off.

Once she accepts and the day is solidified, you can pick the location. Choose a place and tell her the time to meet you by and remember to be firm with your plans no matter what. Asking "Is this place ok?" will make you seem unsure about the whole thing and can potentially make her lose interest. If you ask the right questions beforehand, you will already have an idea of what her likes are and choose a place based on that. If things move fast and you did not have a chance to ask those type of questions, ask what her top three food and drink choices are and choose a location based off that. Except I would highly recommend doing your homework ahead of time and give her the address, name of the location, and tell her to meet you there at a certain time. Doing it that way will not only make you seem assertive, but a woman will be very impressed with actions like that, they will find it sexy and masculine. But most of all, once you decide on a place and time, *never* let her change the day or time on you. If she agreed to meet up Friday at 7:30pm, then its Friday at 7:30pm and nothing else. If she asks to postpone the date for a few hours later, reject her proposal and tell her you prefer not to wait around and say you can plan it for another day. If she specifically asks to postpone for a different day, reject the offer as well and tell her you are busy and will not be able to make it. Also, if you decide to meet and you arrive on time and she is half an hour late or more telling you she is running behind, leave and tell her to have a good night. It is not that hard to get somewhere on time, no one should be left waiting until the other decides to show up. Actions such as those only show how little someone respects your time and how high their interest level is for you at that moment. Yes, sometimes they may have a valid reason because things happen, but that is your judgement call. Some women may be honest on why they need a change of plans, and some do it only for their convenience. It all comes down to your judgment.

    Why is all that important to enforce? It is important because it shows your time is valuable and you are not a pushover. Not only will that raise her respect level with you, but it will show her a glimpse of your value as a man. A lot of women will get other plans presented to them and they will try to change the date for the next day or hours later putting her new plans first. Women know most men will allow her to change everything up to fit what she wants, but you will not let that happen. If you are confused on what to say, tell her anything along the lines of "*We planned this date in advance and I cleared my schedule for it. I prefer to not wait around and I'm busy the rest of the weekend. We can plan for another day, let me know when you're available.*" Anything along those lines is fine, just word it in a way that molds to the context of the situation. Some might think that is harsh to say but doing so will show you actually have balls. Especially if she is changing plans for no good reason or leaves you hanging without warning attempting to offer you a raincheck.

      I will never forget the time I planned this date a full week in advance, and she left me flat without a message or fair warning. We had already gone on a date beforehand, so this was not the first encounter between us. I did not hear from her until she reached out four days later, and her reason was because she got drunk the night before and forgot all about our date. All she said was, "Sorry I forgot, lets reschedule for Saturday night. Sound good?" in a nonchalant manner. Yes, she reached out to reschedule, but what did that show me overall? It showed me she did not take my time serious and did not have the respect to at least let me know she had to cancel. When I responded, I told her exactly what needed to be said. I politely told her my time is valuable and I only give one chance to have it wasted, especially in the way she wasted it. I never showed aggression, nor did I offend her or curse her out, I addressed it in a mature manner. You might say no one owes you anything at the end of the day but I had certain standards and I was not going to lower them for anyone. After that? She began to chase me; she saw I was not like most men who allow themselves to be disrespected and run over. Her indifference and lack of consideration towards me turned into fear of losing her chance with me. My intention was to never see her again, but eventually I gave her a second chance due to her consistent effort and actions. It is safe to say she never left me flat again after that incident, she respected my time and I respected hers. But as you can tell, a simple play such as that can totally change the game with a woman. Showing you are not scared to walk away empty handed will demonstrate your value and let her know you have options. Leading to her pursuing you instead or making sure she does not slip up the next time you plan something. Being stern like that may be uncomfortable at first for some, but the results will undoubtedly benefit you while dating. Actions such as those is the difference between a man they will respect and chase versus a man they will pity and walk all over.

To wrap up, getting her number and having her accept the date is simple, just be direct and confident. Use words of assurance, positivity, and make her feel the excitement of having the opportunity to meet you. Whether she shows signs of direct interest or not, do not let that discourage you from asking, you have nothing to lose especially if she is having a steady conversation with you to begin with. I have successfully landed dates with women who showed obvious signs of romantic interest and ones who barely showed any at all. What matters is the fact that she is actively engaging with you. If she is not, then you are wasting time and energy. That is why it is important to build your female following so you can have options and other choices in case one does not work out. More importantly, always respect a woman's interest towards you and move forward knowing what you bring to the table. Successful dating does not only mean going out on dates, but it is also how you view yourself as a man knowing you are as much of a trophy as she is. As you build and solidify that inner confidence and masculine power and that energy will radiate around you. That will be the moment when you start to notice how women act differently as if there is something about you that makes them go crazy.

Extra Advice:

- ✓ Keep in mind is there are women who do not openly give their personal number out at first. A lot of men can be stalkers with ill intentions, so it is a security thing for some. If you want to play it cool, ask her out on a date first and then ask for her number later once you meet or she openly gives it to you. Do not take a woman who does not give you her number as a sign of rejection, keep going with the flow until her actions or words say otherwise.

Ending Thoughts

There you have it, a step-by-step guide on how to find and date women through Instagram. I am a firm believer that by using these methods, you will be a lot happier with the women you meet. You will be able to meet the type of women you are genuinely attracted to, and not the next best thing you can settle for on a dating platform. We all deserve the good life, and dating beautiful women makes it that much better. Our society year by year is gearing towards online dating more and more, so why not leverage the platforms that everyone uses the most for free? The use of online dating is still in its early stages, and it is not going away anytime soon, probably not even in our lifetime. Use what Instagram gives you for free to your advantage, leverage it as the vehicle to a better dating life. Start using my methods and I promise, you will see positive results and more dates down the line. Never forget to be a man of value and abundance online and in person, I guarantee you that attracting women will become effortless as a result.

Remember to always follow these three affirmations: **I am a man of high value, I am a man of abundance, and I am a man of success.**

No matter who you are, what you do, and what you look like, there will always be plenty of beautiful women for you no matter what. Mistakes will be made, potential dates will be lost, and that is ok! You cannot grow as a person without running into dating hurdles along the way, without it you will never improve your game. That is how you master and polish your craft for the future, remember to learn and grow from every situation moving forward.

- *Cardinal Dating*

Printed in Great Britain
by Amazon